BETWEEN THE WORLD AND ME

Ta-Nehisi Coates

*sparknotes

*sparknotes

SPARKNOTES and the distinctive SparkNotes logo
are registered trademarks of SparkNotes LLC.

© 2020 SparkNotes LLC

This 2020 edition printed for SparkNotes LLC
by Sterling Publishing Co., Inc.

ISBN 978-1-4114-8026-1

Distributed in Canada by Sterling Publishing Co., Inc.
c/o Canadian Manda Group, 664 Annette Street
Toronto, Ontario M6S 2C8, Canada
Distributed in the United Kingdom by GMC Distribution Services
Castle Place, 166 High Street, Lewes, East Sussex BN7 1XU, England
Distributed in Australia by NewSouth Books
University of New South Wales, Sydney, NSW 2052, Australia

For information about custom editions, special sales, and premium
and corporate purchases, please contact Sterling Special Sales at
800-805-5489 or specialsales@sterlingpublishing.com.

Manufactured in Canada

Lot #:
2 4 6 8 10 9 7 5 3 1
09/20

sparknotes.com
sterlingpublishing.com

Please email content@sparknotes.com to report any errors.

CONTENTS

CONTEXT

Ta-Nehisi Coates was born in West Baltimore in 1975. His mother, Cheryl Waters, was a teacher. His father, William Paul Coates, was a publisher who founded the Black Classic Press, which reissued forgotten African American works. His father also worked as a librarian at the Moorland-Spingarn Research Center at Howard University and was a member of the local Black Panther chapter. The neighborhood where Coates grew up was very violent during his childhood. Violence was a common part of daily life, in homes and in the streets. Coates was regularly in fear for his physical safety. However, being surrounded by literature from an early age pushed him to seek answers about the struggles of black people and his culture through reading.

Coates started at Howard University in 1993 but left five years later without a degree. Shortly thereafter, he had his son, Samori, with Kenyatta Matthews, whom he later married. He began to work as a freelance writer, though at first he was not terribly successful. Then he started getting work writing for periodicals. He wrote for *Washington Monthly*, *Philadelphia Weekly*, and *Time*, to name a few. He gained readership when he began corresponding for *The Atlantic* magazine's website. He wrote a series of very opinionated essays that garnered attention, including a few about former president Barack Obama. Coates won a National Magazine Award for two essays written in 2013 and 2014. He was named a MacArthur Fellow in 2015 and earned a PEN/Diamonstein-Spielvogel Award for the Art of the Essay in 2016. Before *Between the World and Me*, Coates published a memoir called *The Beautiful Struggle: A Father, Two Sons, and an Unlikely Road to Manhood*. When he published *Between the World and Me* in 2015, it won the National Book Award and the Kirkus Prize for Nonfiction.

Coates took his inspiration for *Between the World and Me* from James Baldwin, who wrote *The Fire Next Time* in 1963. Baldwin wrote one of the essays in his book as a letter to his nephew, and the subject matter is an analysis of the problems facing African Americans in a time of segregation. Coates's book is a letter to his son concerning much of the same subject matter. When Coates was writing *Between the World and* Me, the issues of police brutality and racial profiling had become prevalent in the media. Coates was profoundly affected by the deaths of unarmed black citizens at the hands of the police.

Between the World and Me references several examples of lethal police brutality. Michael Brown Jr. was an eighteen-year-old black man from Ferguson, Missouri. In 2014, Officer Darren Wilson shot Brown and claimed self-defense, though other witnesses said Brown had his hands up in surrender and was unarmed. The city of Ferguson erupted into riots until the National Guard was called in. Wilson went on trial and was not indicted.

Trayvon Martin was a teenager who was shot and killed by George Zimmerman, the "neighborhood watch captain," in 2012. Zimmerman reported that Trayvon looked suspicious and ignored police instructions to stay in his car and not confront the teenager. Instead, he tracked Trayvon and killed him, claiming self-defense. Zimmerman was acquitted of murder. *Between the World and Me* is Coates's attempt to explain the struggle of black men and women in America to his son—to prepare his son for the realities of his life ahead and pass on his own knowledge gleaned from decades of study. His work serves as a stark eye-opener to issues of racial injustice in the United States.

PLOT OVERVIEW

Between the World and Me is a letter written in three parts. Coates writes directly to his son Samori. Coates is forty years old, and Samori is fifteen. The text is not set up as a traditional narrative. Rather, it traces Coates's thoughts and feelings throughout his life so far. It is a loosely chronological account, though it is sometimes interrupted with anecdotes out of chronological order. The plot has less to do with specific events and more to do with the way Coates's thoughts and opinions changed over time.

Part I begins in the present, as a host for a news show interviews Coates. She asks Coates what it means to lose his body, and he answers her with all the knowledge he has gained over the years. Coates turns to his childhood, describing his life and family as he was growing up in the ghettos of West Baltimore. He first understands the gap between his black world and the suburban white world in childhood, though he cannot articulate the reasons for the separation. Coates begins to give form to his thoughts by reading the many books on Africana that his father owns. He develops a belief system similar to that of Malcolm X and disagrees with the idea of nonviolent protests.

Coates attends Howard University, and his beliefs evolve significantly during this time. He continually studies, reads, and questions everything. He turns to Chancellor Williams' *The Destruction of Black Civilization* as his main guidebook. He begins to think of black people as "kings in exile," severed from their nation by plundering Europeans, and keeps a mental trophy case of African heroes. Debating with older poets and his teachers challenges his views, which leads Coates to journalism. He starts to think about black history more objectively and less romantically. At Howard, he meets Kenyatta Matthews, and she becomes pregnant at twenty-four. He leaves Howard without a degree and moves with Kenyatta to Delaware, where he works as a freelance writer.

The main event in Part II is the murder by police of Prince Jones, whom Coates met at Howard. This is an episode of police brutality in which the officer is not charged. Coates begins to write about Jones's murder and develops a rage at both the police and all of white America. Coates's family moves to New York City in 2001, and Coates finds himself unable to sympathize with the victims of the September 11 terrorist attack because he views them all as part of the system that brought down Prince Jones. Coates describes his life in Brooklyn as a new father with young Samori. His thoughts revolve around Samori understanding the weight and struggle he will have to go through as a black man. The second main event in Part II is a trip to France. Travel opens Coates's eyes to worlds outside of America. He realizes how much fear has damaged his life and is able to better place himself in the larger context of the world as a whole.

In Part III, Coates visits Prince Jones's mother, Dr. Mable Jones. He is amazed by her composure and compares it to the steady determination of his grandmother and the protestors at sit-ins in the 1960s. Dr. Jones speaks about her own history and tells Coates more about Prince. After leaving, Coates sits in his car and rethinks his views of nonviolent protestors. He used to think they were shameful not to fight for themselves, but he now believes they may have known that there was never any security to fight for in the first place. He reflects on attending Howard University's homecoming and the sense of black power he felt within that group of people. His parting message to his son is to remind Samori to engage fully in the struggle of his life as a black person, but to know he is not responsible for converting white people to the struggle. Coates is confident that white America will continue to plunder not only black bodies but the environment, too. The text thus begins and ends discussing the white assault against the black body.

CHARACTER LIST

Ta-Nehisi Coates The author and Samori's father. Coates is a dynamic intellectual with passionate opinions about being black in America, which change and evolve over the course of the book. His childhood in the ghettos of West Baltimore serves as the backdrop for all his later experiences.

Samori Coates Coates's fifteen-year-old son, to whom the book is written. Coates makes it clear that their childhoods are different. Samori was raised in Brooklyn and has traveled with his father. Because of his environment, Samori has experienced less fear than Coates, but still recognizes the same gap between black and white that his father did.

Kenyatta Matthews Coates's wife, whom Coates only refers to as "your mother." She meets Coates at Howard and engenders key changes within Coates, such as teaching him how to be a loving father and sharing her love of travel. She inspires him to move to New York City and travel to Paris, which provides Coates a wider perspective on the world.

Prince Jones Coates's contemporary at Howard who was murdered by police. His murder has a serious impact on Coates and darkens his view toward the police and all of white America.

Dr. Mable Jones Prince Jones' mother and a radiologist. She is the central character in Part III, when Coates visits her years after Prince's murder. Coates respects her composure and determination to break the poverty cycle and give her children an excellent life.

Uncle Ben and Aunt Janai Close friends of the Coates family (not blood relatives). Coates meets Uncle Ben at Howard and refers to him as a fellow searcher.

CHARACTER LIST

Girl with the dreadlocks An unnamed, bisexual love interest for Coates at Howard. She challenges Coates's prejudicial views towards bisexual and gay people and is the first to show him true tenderness. She teaches him that love is heroic, but does not return Coates's interest romantically.

Samori's paternal grandparents Coates's mother and father. Coates refers to them anecdotally and says their love was hard, not tender. Coates's father once worked as a librarian at Howard, and he provided Coates with many books from a young age.

Samori's maternal grandmother Coates's mother-in-law. She makes an impression on Coates when she tells him to take care of her daughter, Kenyatta. She helps Coates realize the magnitude of his responsibility as a partner and father.

News show host Interviewer for a popular news show. Her interview with Coates opens the book, and by the end, she still does not seem to fully grasp his point about black bodies. Her lack of understanding represents the larger whole of America.

ANALYSIS OF MAJOR CHARACTERS

TA-NEHISI COATES

As the author, Coates is the main character, and he is the only character whose thoughts the reader has direct insight into. Coates is a very dynamic and intellectual person. His viewpoints and moral schema change several times over the course of his life. Through the letter to his son, the reader sees his world open further and further from childhood, to university, to partnership and fatherhood, to travel and a thriving career. As the author, he allows an unusually vulnerable insight into his mind. This vulnerability is furthered by the fact that he is not trying to talk to the reader. Instead, he is speaking directly to his son, Samori. In so doing, Coates has no need to sugarcoat events or to placate an audience. This unique personal letter-based approach allows him to express views that could be offensive to white readers. If the letter were addressed to white Americans, they might feel attacked and put the text down. But writing to his son provides a degree of separation that may translate into getting white people to listen with some degree of compassion, as parenthood is a common human experience. Coates does not withhold thoughts that he believes Samori needs to know.

One of Coates's most important character traits is his willingness to let others challenge his ideas. For this, Coates likely has his parents to thank. Between his mother teaching him to read at a young age and his father providing plentiful books, Coates was consistently exposed to different viewpoints. Curiosity is another of Coates's defining traits. His intense curiosity rendered him bored with the mundanity of school and likely led to his troubles both in grade school and at Howard University. Coates left Howard without a degree, but having read many books, because he was interested in satiating his curiosity more than taking part in organized classes. He also found his passion for journalism, which enabled him to ask questions that mattered to him. Coates demonstrates that, to him, education is about the quest for knowledge, not passing classes. Overall, he provides an array of thoughts that are at once honest and angry, direct and eloquent.

Samori Coates

As the recipient of Coates's letter, Samori is a major character, but the reader has no knowledge of Samori's thoughts; there are only a couple instances that give insight into Samori's character. Coates writes about the week that the police officer who killed Michael Brown is set free. Coates says that Samori is still young at this time, so he believes that justice will be done. When it isn't, Samori goes to his room and cries. This is potentially a defining moment in Samori's life. Coates hints this may have been when Samori first realizes that despite his relatively privileged life, he is still a young black man and this reality will affect how the world treats him.

Coates describes taking Samori to preschool and Samori immediately running off to play with the other children. He doesn't fear rejection; he simply embraces the new experience. Coates admires Samori for his outgoing personality. Through this recollection, the reader can see that Samori has lived more unafraid than his father. This fearlessness is due to Samori's privileged household, his ability to travel, and his parents' investment in his upbringing.

Dr. Mable Jones

Dr. Mable Jones is the mother of Prince Jones and appears in the third section of the book. She is reserved, polite, composed, and incredibly determined. Coates presents Dr. Jones as a woman of steel who was born into poverty and fought her way out by winning scholarships and becoming a doctor. She gave the very best to her children and earned the money to do so. She is the epitome of being "twice as good," a phrase Coates describes as being doled out to black children and not white children. Despite having fought her way to the top in spite of segregation and prejudice, Dr. Jones does not acknowledge that she was ever bothered at being the only black radiologist she knew, revealing her commitment to keeping insecurity from holding her back. She believes that it should not be notable for her to be a black doctor; she just wants to be a good doctor, on her own merits. Her composure also belies the immense struggle she has gone through in losing Prince. Coates describes her as having the same look in her eye that he had seen in photos of 1960s sit-in demonstrators. She gains her power from something greater than herself. As a woman who survived extreme prejudice and the violent loss of her child, Dr. Jones exemplifies sheer strength.

KENYATTA MATTHEWS

Though Coates provides little insight into Samori's mother, Kenyatta is still a very important character. Coates was drawn to her because she understands the concept of cosmic injustice. She is a searcher, like him. When they meet at Howard, she knows more of the world than Coates, acting as a bridge between Coates and worldly knowledge. She grew up without a father and gives Coates a new insight into how a woman fears for her body in ways that a man does not. She is both a gentle and adventurous character, evidenced by her treatment of Samori and her travel experiences. She teaches Coates how to be gentle with Samori, and she gives both Coates and Samori a softer love that Coates did not experience with his own parents. Kenyatta's solo trip to Paris demonstrates her strength, and she transmits this adventurous spirit to Coates. Her importance as a character lies in the ways that she changes Coates and makes him a better man and father.

THEMES, MOTIFS & SYMBOLS

THEMES

Themes are the fundamental and often universal ideas explored in a literary work.

THE FAÇADE OF THE AMERICAN DREAM

Between the World and Me demonstrates how the American Dream is built on the enslavement of the African people and their oppression by violent means. Coates first mentions the Dream when he says that the television news host asks him to "awaken her from the most gorgeous dream" by inquiring about his body. He describes the Dream as cookouts, nice lawns, Cub Scouts, and strawberry shortcake, among other things. Coates first realized that there was a painfully obvious gap between himself and his counterparts in the white suburbs when he first saw young white boys living the American Dream on television.

Coates speaks about how white Americans deify democracy and think there is some preordained glory about America, as if it is the greatest and noblest country because of its democratic and justice systems. However, Coates purports that this white concept of American democracy is a lie because the slaves were disregarded and not counted as people. He says that the country has swept slavery under the rug, touting hard-working Americans as the key to a successful nation. As Coates shows Samori at the Civil War battlefields, slaves and their labor in the cotton industry is what truly gave America its foundation. The legacy of the war was then turned into Westerns, reenactments, and displays of weaponry. Thus, it is very difficult for white Americans today, removed from the actions of slave owners, to admit that America is not innocent and is in fact built on atrocities committed against other humans. The very foundation of the American Dream is shaken when considered through black eyes.

The Destruction of the Black Body

Racism toward black people is centered on forcibly taking away physical control of the black person's body. This began with slavery, as Coates describes in visceral detail on more than one occasion. He emphasizes that it is easy to view slavery as a mass of black people in cotton fields, but he urges Samori to consider each individual slave as a person, and then to realize that that person was physically tortured into labor. This abuse continued into the Civil Rights Movement, with lynchings and tear gas and water hoses used as an assault on black bodies.

Coates explains throughout the book how the destruction of the black body is still prevalent today. While this destruction is readily evident to a black person, it is often much less obvious to a white person, especially the "Dreamers" who are not experiencing persistent racism. Coates describes growing up in the ghettos of Baltimore and how those sorts of neighborhoods across the country are meant to be filled with black people. Segregation is not legal, but government policy ensures it happens anyway. Coates's neighborhood was very violent, and he (and everyone else) was in constant fear for his body because it could be taken from him at any time. He first truly understands this when a boy pulls a gun on him for no reason. He never had real security over his body. Another clear example of the destruction of the black body is the regularity of police brutality and how often it ends in murder, without any consequence for the police officer responsible. Coates references many black persons killed by police, including his friend Prince Jones, Michael Brown, and Trayvon Martin.

The Value of the Struggle

While emotionally exhausting, struggling to honestly understand oneself in the larger context of race is more valuable than living in ignorance. Coates tells Samori that his entire life has been dedicated to wondering how he can live freely in America with his black body, knowing the brutalities that America has committed against black people. Then Coates says that "the question is unanswerable, which is not to say futile," and that his constant grappling with this question has helped him to cope with the fear of having his body taken from him. In fact, he tells Samori that the "Struggle" is all Coates has to give him.

Coates classifies himself as a searcher and begins reading at age four. He reads his father's books about Africana throughout his childhood. At Howard University, he reads copious amounts of

THEMES

books to research African history and viewpoints, which he finds all contradict one another. He describes all this searching as a struggle that weighs him down, but he cannot stop. By the end of his time at Howard, Coates realizes that the point of his education is to leave him in discomfort, allowing him to see the world in its truth.

MOTIFS

Motifs are recurring structures, contrasts, or literary devices that can help to develop and inform the text's major themes.

VIOLENCE

Violence is present throughout *Between the World and Me*. One of Coates's main points in his letter is to impress upon Samori how white America has systematically destroyed black bodies in a violent way. In the past, slavery was the means of oppression, and today, violence is most present in police brutality and mass incarceration. He explains how the violence against black people in the past led to violence in the streets today, calling the streets "killing grounds." He also describes his childhood as being violent, both with other people in the streets and within his own family. He speaks about violence during the Civil War and the Civil Rights Movement. Nonviolence does not make as much sense to him as the views of Malcom X or the Black Panthers. He also speaks specifically about violence in the death of his friend Prince Jones, who was a victim of racist police violence. Ultimately, Coates asserts that no black person has ever or will ever be safe from the consistent threat of violence in the United States.

DREAMERS

After initially describing what "Dreamers" are, Coates uses the term to describe white America as a whole, due to the white obsession with the American Dream. Because Coates has spent his life trying to understand the gap between himself as a black person and the people who ignore slavery and see America as great and noble, the concept of the American Dream and the Dreamers recurs often. He tells Samori it is not his responsibility to convert the Dreamers and make them see their errors. While at first Coates himself desired the American Dream, the more he studies, the more he realizes that he wants to understand the United States as it truly is, even if that makes him a realist who is wide awake, rather than a Dreamer.

FEAR

Fear is arguably the most prevalent motif in *Between the World and Me*, and this prevalence underscores the ways that fear permeates all of black society. Coates describes how fears centered in past oppression and the current lack of security over one's body drives fear into the streets, and that fear drives further violence. He was always afraid as a child because he knew he could be killed at any time. He experiences constant fear for Samori because he knows that, as a black man, Samori will have a higher risk of being beaten or killed. Coates is afraid of the police, which he mentions directly when he is stopped by a cop. As a parent, he also comes to understand his own parents' fear for their child's safety. The only place Coates doesn't feel the same fear is in Paris, because the French don't have the same tradition of violence against black people. Though fear remains manifest in the black experience, Coates has provided Samori with a life filled with significantly more security than his own.

SYMBOLS

Symbols are objects, characters, figures, or colors used to represent abstract ideas or concepts.

THE YARD

The Yard at Howard University—the popular gathering place at the center of campus—represents the diversity of the black race. While looking out over the Yard, Coates calls Howard "the black diaspora." He sees black people from all over the world. They study different things, look exotic, and all have different styles. He never met such a diverse pool of people in the relatively homogenous ghettos of Baltimore. When Coates references the Yard, he is referencing not just memories of that specific meeting place, but also the diverse group of people gathered there and the beautiful complexity of his race.

PARIS

To Coates, Paris represents security over one's body. When he travels to Paris for the first time, he realizes that he is free from the constant fear of being assaulted that he experiences daily in America. Unlike white Americans, the French have never systematically enslaved Africans. He isn't looked upon with any prejudice or suspicion resulting from his race, which is something he has never experienced. Coates takes Samori to Paris because he wants him to experience life without that fear and to enjoy security in a new way.

Summary & Analysis

Part I, Pages 5–13

Summary

Between the World and Me is a letter that Ta-Nehisi Coates writes to his teenage son Samori. Coates begins by describing an interview he did for a news podcast. The host asks Coates what it means to "lose his body" and why he thinks that white America's progress is built on looting and violence. Coates clarifies that white America is really "those Americans who believe they are white." His short answer is that American history explains white America's progress. Then he gives a complex overview of American history and its relationship to race, racism, and the violent physical extortion of black peoples' bodies. He believes Americans have made democracy into a god and use it to forgive themselves of the nation's enslavement and torture of black people. When Abraham Lincoln declared everlasting "government of the people, for the people, and by the people" in his 1863 Gettysburg Address, the country did not define black individuals as people.

When Coates finishes his attempt at an explanation, the host shows a picture of a black child hugging a white police officer and asks Coates whether there is hope. At this moment, Coates is sad because he knows he has failed to articulate his point. He has to search internally to understand why he is feeling saddened. The host is essentially asking him to awaken her from the "dream" of an innocent America and its white culture. He realizes his sadness is for all the people who are brought up believing they are white and reveling in superficial hope. However, he is mostly sad for Samori. Though Coates himself has long wished he could escape into this dream, it is not possible for black people because the dream itself rests on their backs.

Coates writes to his son when Samori is fifteen. In this year, Samori has seen several cases of undeserved police brutality against black individuals. Samori now understands that police have been given the authority to destroy his body. Coates reminds Samori that this is the week he learns that the killer of Michael Brown will go free. Samori stays up to watch the indictment and upon learning the police officer will go unpunished, goes to his room and cries. Coates sits with Samori but doesn't try to comfort him, instead telling him the reality of the situation. This is his country, he is in a black body, and he has to figure out how to live with it. At any point, a black person's body can be destroyed or assaulted for any reason, and the guilty parties are rarely held responsible.

Coates has spent his whole life trying to figure out how to live in a black body in the midst of the American Dream. His parents taught him to reject the idea that America had a preordained glory and never consoled him with a belief in religion or an afterlife. Accepting that this is his only life, he asks: "How do I live freely within this black body?" He has sought to answer this question through reading, writing, music, arguments, and school, and has concluded that it is unanswerable. However, his constant struggle to come to grips with the brutality of his nation and his lack of control over his own body have freed him from his biggest fear—disembodiment. In this way, the struggling and questioning is worthwhile, though Coates knows there is no answer.

ANALYSIS

The first several pages of Coates's letter set the tone and basis of his viewpoint. He introduces ideas of "those who believe they are white" and "the Dream," which seem opaque at first, but Coates considers them to be an essential part of America's history. Coates posits that Americans think of "race" as one's inherent feature, given to them by Mother Nature. "Racism" is the need to assign this feature (color) to people and then use it to humiliate or destroy them. Therefore, Americans widely believe that racism follows race. But if race is inherent, this allows people to view racism as an unfortunate external consequence of Mother Nature—like a natural disaster—instead of man's handiwork. Coates argues that racism actually comes before race. Deciding who counts as a person doesn't depend on genes or physical features but on the belief that these features can indicate a hierarchy within society. Humans have always had different hair and eye colors, but it is a newer belief that these differences can indicate how to correctly organize a society or can decide who has more and less worth.

This new idea is at the heart of a group of people who have been brought up to believe that they are white. But "white" as a race in America doesn't really mean anything. All white people were named something else before they were named white, such as Catholic or

Welsh. Those who believe they are white are those who grew up in a nation founded on the belief that it had a right to choose which inherent traits indicated a correct ordering of society. Coates says that unlike "black," the term "white" is tied to criminal power. The "elevation of the belief of being white"—white progress—has nothing to do with the things that are culturally associated with white people in America. White progress isn't innovation, Memorial Day cookouts, or football. White progress has been accomplished through violent acts against slaves. Coates emphasizes that all our current phrases to describe this problem—such as racial profiling, racial justice, and white privilege—are all meant to obscure that the problem is really physical, visceral violence against black bodies.

Coates points out that this problem isn't unique to America. All powerful nations have become powerful in part by violently exploiting others' bodies and forcing them into labor. However, Coates believes America should be held to a higher moral standard because America claims that it is a great and noble champion because of its democracy. This claim is hypocritical because slave labor "built" America, and that is not real democracy. Now, many white Americans in the generations after slavery do believe slavery is wrong and reject the idea that race has anything to do with a human's worth. However, it is much easier for white people to ignore the past and believe that the current America is innocent of the sins of the past. Coates contends it is not sufficient to disconnect oneself from the dead white people who perpetrated slavery.

Applying a truly moral standard would mean facing and questioning the evil things that our nation has done, and it would be painful. It would mean accepting the fact that today's white individuals are still profiting from past evils and cannot be declared innocent. Meanwhile, black people cannot turn a blind eye to America's history simply because the injustice was committed against their ancestors. Slavery persists today in the form of fear for one's body. Coates says the American Dream is the naïve or willfully ignorant belief that America is now innocent and forgiven of its past. For Americans who believe they are white, the Dream is a blissful lie.

PART I, PAGES 14–39

SUMMARY

*"Good intention" is a hall pass through history, a
sleeping pill that ensures the Dream.*

(See QUOTATIONS, *p. 39)*

Coates realizes fear has been present his whole life, and looking
back, he recognizes that all the displays of power in his black community were born out of fear: the dramatic clothing of the gangs in
his neighborhood, the loud music, the loud women, and the hard
and brutal stares. They are all attempts to assert control. He also
sees fear in his family, especially in his father, who beats him with
a belt. Coates tells a story about his mother and grandmother. His
mother let a man in the house who claimed to be his grandmother's
boyfriend, and when his grandmother got home, she made the man
leave and then beat his mother harshly. It was an effort to remind
Coates's mother how easily she could lose her body. His own father
beats Coates when he is a child and later claims either he can beat
his son, or the police can.

This parental violence comes from both fear and love, but children take that same violence to the streets. Coates speaks of his
youth in West Baltimore as being "naked." His body is constantly
vulnerable. An older boy pulls a gun on him for no reason. The boy
doesn't shoot, but Coates suddenly understands just how easily his
body can be taken from him and begins to understand the city's
frequent murders. Contrary to his daily experience, Coates sees a
different world on TV. There, white boys don't constantly fear for
their bodies, and life seems to consist of suburbs, cookouts, and
football cards. He recognizes even as a child that his life is a world
away from the lives on TV and that there is an insurmountable difference between black fear and white freedom, though he doesn't
know why this is the case. He wants to escape the fear of his world.

Coates resents the school system because it is just a new way to
control the body. Being a good student means keeping one's head
down, working quietly, and walking in straight lines. The schools
praise the nonviolence of the Civil Rights Movement, but, to Coates,
the black protestors just seem like they love getting hurt. It doesn't
make sense to him to put these protestors on a pedestal when the
same behavior in the streets will get one killed. He sees the streets

and school as "two arms of the same beast." If you don't do well in the streets, you get hurt, and if you don't do well in school, they send you back to the streets, where you get hurt. Coates warns that intentions do not matter because good intentions allow people to shirk responsibility for their actions.

Coates does not have religion to take solace in or help him answer questions, so he turns to writing and books, of which his father has many. He is drawn to Malcom X because Malcolm X is straight-forward, honest about his emotions, and wholly concerned with protecting the black body. He has no interest in fake morality or meekness. Coates relates to Malcolm X because he too was almost killed on the streets and clashed with the school system. Coates admires that Malcolm X "found himself" by reading in prison, and when he got out, he spoke and acted like someone in control of his own body. Coates finds hope that he can feel this freedom through study and exploration.

ANALYSIS

Coates's portrait of growing up on the streets explains the cyclical fear which filled his childhood, and this is evident in his father say-ing: "Either I beat him, or the police." His father knows that the police have regularly used the authority of the law to beat or kill black men, and he views it as a better alternative for him to do the beating instead of the police. Coates has already referenced sev-eral cases of police violence for Samori. Coates says that using the authority of the law to harm black bodies comes from the tradition of slavery. Even though black people are legally free, the reality is that it is permissible to physically put them in their place without repercussion, especially when a police officer is involved. Coates's father knows that it would take very little for Coates to be seriously harmed by police. A wrong movement, wrong word, or just being near the wrong address at the wrong time could cost him his life. So his father, reacting out of fear and love, pelts Coates to physically show him how easy it is to lose the security of one's body. He wants to beat discipline into him because he is scared of losing him.

This fear seeps into the streets, too. Young people's parents beat them, so they are afraid of their parents as well as afraid of the police, and the kids themselves are violent with each other. Learning the culture of the streets is a daily effort to avoid violence and secure Coates's own body. The body language, phrases, movements, and gang relationships that Coates must memorize leave so little room for error that they practically guarantee violence and crime. The gangs in his neighborhood dress in clothes that suggest authority and fight on the streets according to complex codes and bylaws. Their baggy clothes, puffy jackets, and chains are meant to assert control so nobody can touch them. The same is true for loud music and loud, aggressive women. Coates can now see through these actions and knows that trying to appear powerful is just a shield from the fear of the violence against their past generations.

Coates says that school is part of the same beast as the streets. Society teaches Coates that school is a place where you can avoid jail. Coates struggles with school, which seems ironic because he is clearly a very curious child. But the schools are not concerned with the curiosities of black boys and girls. Being a good student truly means letting the school have more control over the body. In contrast white schools don't say "this will keep you out of jail," but instead "this will get you into college." In white schools, education is viewed as a stepping-stone to pursue one's interests and obtain a fulfilling job.

The streets are like a trap that Coates and his community cannot escape. He describes his father beating him both for letting another boy steal from him and for yelling at a teacher. Coates learns that one can have their body assaulted if they are either not violent enough or too violent, and this produces constant fear. The schools have no answer as to how the knowledge they teach that seems completely irrelevant to Coates's daily life could make a difference for a black boy or girl.

PART I, PAGES 39–57

SUMMARY

> It began to strike me that the point of my education
> was a kind of discomfort, was the process that would
> not award me my own especial Dream but would
> break all the dreams, all the comforting myths of
> Africa, of America, and everywhere, and would leave
> me only with humanity in all its terribleness.
>
> (See QUOTATIONS, p. 39)

Coates talks about his alma mater, Howard University, which he calls his Mecca. Howard is a historically black college in Washington, DC. There, Coates sees a beautiful, diverse assembly of black people from exotic places and different backgrounds. He calls it "the cross-roads of the black diaspora." He feels all of black history walk-ing through the campus. Howard is a place where black history feels important, whereas the important historical figures he learned about in school were all white. Furthermore, Howard is located in a place of political power, and he walks in the footsteps of his heroes. He begins to think about black history as a thing of its own, rooted in Africa, complete with powerful scientists and cultural heroes.

Coates spends much time in the Moorland-Spingarn Research Center, where his father once worked. It contains an incredible amount of writings by and about black people. Coates requests three books in the morning and spends the day reading and then writing his thoughts. He yearns to learn all he can about black his-tory and thinks that if he can just read enough, he will discover a unified story. However, he finds that histories are presented differ-ently, and authors often contradict each other. He is drawn to the library rather than the classroom because he can pursue his own curiosities freely.

Coates meets other people searching for answers, among them Samori's Uncle Ben, whom Coates becomes close friends with. Coates writes poetry and performs it at open mic nights, and there he meets older poets who introduce him to more poetry and make him question his own writing and thinking. Coates begins to admire poetry in the same way he admires Malcolm X. sPoetry can say much about something without ever stating anything outright. He spends nights arguing and debating with these poets. Because of these inter-actions and so much reading, Coates wants to learn to write. He recognizes writing as a method to confront his own innocence and rationalizations. Coates realizes that the point of his education is to learn to live in a constant state of mental chaos and questioning, designed to leave him in discomfort by breaking all myths about The Dream and simply laying out the terribleness of the world.

Coates assures Samori that being black doesn't make one immune to doing bad things and warns him to be careful not to get sucked into any nation's dream. In Prince George county, black police who have been sucked into the white dream turn into the same plunder-ers who perpetuate violence under the guise of the law. Coates's his-tory teachers challenge him to rethink his ideas about black nobility and not confuse political propaganda with hard study. He rethinks his idea about having a black "trophy case" of solely black intel-lectuals, as if they are better because they have not fallen prey to the

Dream and are in control of their own bodies. Upon taking a class about Europe, Coates sees how "white" Irish people are treated in a similar way to those who lose their bodies to slavery, and he wonders if being "black" actually has nothing to do with losing his body, but whether the term just means his race is at the bottom of the totem pole. He is certainly part of a tribe, but perhaps that tribe does not possess the romanticism that he once believed.

ANALYSIS

This section represents the largest bloom of Coates's intellectual investigation. He finally makes it off the streets, out of childhood, and away from the schools that don't care about his curiosity. Howard University is a place where he can devote all the time he wants to learning and satiating his questions. He starts the description of the university by calling Howard his Mecca. He assumes that the reader knows the meaning of Mecca, which is a place that draws people to itself, and, when capitalized, refers to the birthplace of Muhammed, the holiest city for Muslims. Knowing this definition helps clarify what Howard means to Coates. Coates has already stated he does not believe in God, but he does believe in constantly pursuing knowledge and an understanding about himself as a black person in America. Therefore, Howard is his personal Mecca, the holiest place in his search for answers. In "the black diaspora," he sees people from his personal heritage who have dispersed and populated different parts of the world. After seeing gangs in the projects and learning only about white leaders, he finally meets black individuals who pursue all sorts of intellectual subjects and come from different states and countries. He also walks in the footsteps, literally and metaphorically, of his black heroes.

At Howard, Coates grows to define himself as a searcher and a struggler. His days in the Moorland-Spingarn Research Center are critical to his growth as a person because he inhales ideas and opinions from myriad authors and then analyzes his thoughts about them. When he describes seeing the diversity of people on the campus, he experiences a reflection of what he has read in the library. Even as they are all black in his eyes, they have different backgrounds and opinions. When he begins writing poetry, it is not for the sake of performance but for investigation. Through all these days spent in the library, he recognizes that writing is the best form of personal investigation; writing insists that you figure out what you really mean and why you mean it. Writing affords Coates the opportunity to meet other poets, all of whom are, like him, searching for where they fit in the world. These poets and his teachers challenge him and lead him to read even more. They force him to be specific and critical about his own work and thoughts.

Coates experiences two significant paradigm shifts in this section. He initially wants to understand just how the African people are separated from their roots. As he reads about people of power and significance in Africa, he sees that his race has its own scientists, musicians, writers, and engineers. He develops a mental trophy case of his African heroes and, after a time, begins to think of black people as nobility. They are all kings in exile from their native lands, forcibly severed from their roots. During this period when he looks out on the Yard, he sees beautiful kings and queens with precious black bodies. But as time progresses and he speaks with the poets and his teachers, he realizes he is falling into a Dream of his own making. He has romanticized Africa and his heritage, just as he accuses Americans of romanticizing theirs.

PART I, PAGES 57–71

SUMMARY

Coates describes falling in love. He first falls in love with a woman from Bangladesh, and she opens his eyes to the vastness of the world. He calls her black out of ignorance because it is all he knows to call her. She opens a wormhole for him because she has traveled to and carried the lineage of distant lands. Coates then falls in love with a bisexual woman with long dreadlocks, who lives with a bisexual Howard professor and his wife. This woman teaches him a form of love that is softer than his parents' love. He reminisces about the first time he has a migraine, and she brings him to her house to take care of him.

Coates admires the way black people dance. He wants to dance, but a fear of his body has always held him back. Watching the people dance uninhibited in clubs, he appreciates that music and rhythm allow them to exhibit complete control of their bodies. He compares their dancing to Malcolm X's voice. This spurs his desire to write in the way that they dance, with control, power, joy, and warmth. He publishes articles and reviews in alternative newspapers, and his teachers edit them. The teachers point him toward journalism, which he loves because it enables him to ask questions. Coates speaks briefly about a young man named Prince Jones, whom he loves because Prince is generous, kind, and warm. He foreshadows that Prince will die at a young age.

Coates meets Samori's mother, Kenyatta, at Howard. She is from Chicago and has no father. Like Coates, she seems aware of cosmic injustices. Furthermore, he recognizes that she understands the type of injustice against female bodies that he can never experience. She becomes pregnant with Samori; the pregnancy is unplanned, and they are unmarried. Samori holds them together because they are both aware of the protection they owe their child. When they leave Howard, Coates has not completed his degree and instead works as a freelance writer. Samori's grandmother comes to visit them during the pregnancy and tells Coates to take care of Kenyatta, her only daughter. Coates says his world changes at that moment because he realizes he is responsible for his family. Samori is named after Samori Toure, who resisted French colonizers and died in captivity. Coates intentionally names Samori after someone who struggled for freedom because Coates believes that there is a lot of wisdom in the struggle. One of the most important lessons he learns from the streets is that one's tribe struggles and fights together, whatever the outcome.

Coates encourages Samori to remember slaves as individuals, not simply as a mass of people. Each slave has their own personality, dreams, and family. Coates tells Samori to never forget that black people in America were enslaved longer than they have been free, and generations of individuals knew nothing but chains. Lastly, he emphasizes that no matter how improved the current situation of the black race is, it is not redemption for the enslavement of generations that came before. It isn't Samori's responsibility to change the world. While it is a beautiful world, he will still have to struggle with how to exist in his black body.

Analysis

The different loves that Coates experiences at Howard help him reevaluate himself and his own ignorance. He describes kissing the woman from Bangladesh as opening up a mental wormhole. He can only name her "black" because he doesn't know what else to call her, but she is a different black than him and has been to distant lands. She functions essentially as an expansion of his worldview. Being with this woman allows Coates to have an even more intimate experience with the knowledge of other lands. The fact that she carries a different lineage and heritage make him feel ignorant in her presence, but Coates, having already identified himself as a searcher, is drawn to identifying his ignorance because it presents an opportunity to learn.

The bisexual girl with the dreadlocks changes Coates's view of love, though she doesn't appear to return his romantic feelings. He has been raised in an environment that is prejudiced against queer people and has spent his life calling them names and hating them. This woman, who uses her sexuality to take and express control of her own body, convinces him to change his views. The question of Coates's life is how to feel free in his body. This woman seems to feel secure and at peace in hers, but she is controlling her body in a way that he has been taught is perverse. He feels torn between judging her and the bisexual couple she lives with, and being jealous of their closeness and bodily security. When he gets a migraine, the woman exhibits more tender love than he has ever felt. The more time he spends with them, the less his prejudices make sense to him. He realizes that in the same way he thinks of white people plundering his body, perhaps he has also stolen from gay and bisexual people of his own race.

We can see Coates's thoughts shift when he meets Kenyatta and she becomes pregnant with Samori. Until that point, he has been primarily concerned with his own personal explorations and questions, but when Samori's mother becomes pregnant, he feels very young. They aren't married at the time, but Samori keeps them together. They both know that they owe as much protection to their child as they can give him. The reader can infer that this realization is connected to the lack of security and protection that Coates and Kenyatta felt their whole lives. Coates now understands that the security of his family partially falls under his control and that if he fails at his ventures in life, his family will go down with him. Samori's maternal grandmother puts this in stark light when she comes to visit and directly tells Coates to take care of her only daughter. From here on out, Coates's intellectual exploration is not just about his own questions but about passing information to his son. Specifically, it is about getting Samori to understand that the value of life is in the struggle itself.

PART II, PAGES 75–88

SUMMARY

*I believed, and still do, that our bodies are our selves,
that my soul is the voltage conducted through neurons
and nerves, and that my spirit is my flesh.*
                                             (See QUOTATIONS, *p. 40)*

Part II of *Between the World and Me* opens with Coates describing an instance where he is stopped by PG (Prince George) County police on the side of the road. As he waits for the officer, he is terrified. Even though the police force is mostly black, they have a reputation for police brutality. Sitting in the car, Coates thinks of all the violent incidences he has heard of in PG County. Despite FBI investigations into the force, officers largely go unpunished and are sent back out onto the streets. That night, the officer leaves without offering a reason for the stop, and this reminds Coates how easily he might lose his body for nothing.

Later, Coates reads that PG police have killed Prince Jones, his friend from Howard. Over the next weeks, Coates discovers that the police were supposed to have been following a man of significantly differing physical description, and instead they tracked Prince through three states to Virginia, where he was driving to visit his fiancée. There were no witnesses, and the cop claimed self-defense and shot him. There was no evidence to support a self-defense claim and virtually no investigation into the officer, who was not punished. Coates and his wife go to Prince's funeral on Howard's campus. Coates feels distanced from all the other mourners. Prince was a born-again Christian, and the pastor prays for forgiveness for the shooter. But that does not move Coates because he does not believe there is a God and cannot participate in prayer. He also feels that forgiving the single officer is futile, because the officer alone is not the murderer. The entire country and its systems are also responsible because the killer only expresses his country's beliefs.

Prince's death increases Coates's fears for Samori. Prince had successfully escaped the ghettos which consumed so many, moved on to higher education, and actively lived out his Christian faith, but none of this saved him from getting killed. Coates urges Samori to think about all the effort, investment, and love that Prince's family poured into him over the years. Coates begins to write about Prince's death, investigating the PG County police through the new tool of the internet. Politicians tell Coates that the community prefers "safety" and the preservation of order, and they are unlikely to complain about police brutality. After Prince's death, Coates has one dream about him. In the dream, Coates wants to warn Prince about the plunderers, but Prince shakes his head and turns away.

Coates has never considered living anywhere other than Baltimore after school, simply because he cannot imagine it for himself. However, he comes to realize that other people look farther out into the world searching for meaning, such as Kenyatta and Uncle Ben. Through culture and TV, Samori's mother falls in love with New York, so the Coates family moves there when she gets a job in the city. At the time, Coates makes almost no money as a freelance writer. On September 11, 2001, Coates looks out at the destruction and is unable to sympathize with America or even the police officers and firefighters who lose their lives. The demonstrations of flags and American pride seem ridiculous to him because he cannot see a difference between the police officers at Ground Zero and the police officer who killed Prince. They do not seem human to Coates, only dangerous forces of nature that can steal his body.

ANALYSIS

This section comprises the darkest part of the letter and Coates's thoughts. Prince's death gives birth to a burning rage. Coates knows firsthand how difficult it is for a black person to get off the streets and break the cycle of poverty. Though he doesn't know Prince's precise background, it is clear from his attendance at Howard that Prince had a community of support and that people had invested in him. He and his family had escaped the streets, and he had mastered the schools. He had a fiancée and by all accounts was a kind and warm Christian person. He was, as black parents told their children to be, "twice as good." If a man such as Prince can still be murdered and forgotten, then so can Coates and so can Samori. Prince's death leads Coates to an insight into his own parents' fear. He suddenly understands how his father had been so fearful that he beat his own son and why his mother held his hand so tightly when they crossed the street. They understood that their only child and legacy could be taken in a moment. Furthermore, nobody would be held accountable, and a black person's death would be ascribed to "race," not human fault.

Coates urges Samori to consider how it was not only Prince's body that was plundered but also all the effort and love that had been poured into him. This reveals much about how Coates views the black body. By considering all the lost effort and love when Prince dies, Coates does not think of a body as just flesh and blood, but instead as a vessel for that person's family, their ancestors, and all the history contained therein. This is why Coates views the black body as so precious. He realizes that his own parents view him as their legacy, and he sees Samori that way as well. Especially given that Coates does not believe in God or an afterlife and cannot connect with the idea that Prince is with Jesus during his funeral, it makes sense that the physical body is of the highest importance because it is the ultimate vessel and connection to the rest of the world.

Coates's anger over Prince's death pushes him to a painful point on September 11, 2001, after the terrorist attacks on the World Trade Center in New York City. He describes his heart as being cold, and he cannot feel sympathy for the first responders in his new city. This may seem contradictory at first, given that Coates has told Samori to look at groups of victims in a very individual, detailed way instead of as a racially defined group. After all, Prince had been shot by a black cop in a black neighborhood. However, Coates cannot feel sympathy for the first responders or for America as a whole because during that period, for him, the country is split into Dreamers and those oppressed by the Dream. The white people enslaved black people and built the American Dream on black backs. After slavery was abolished, fear permeated the segregated black communities all the way into the present. Fear seeps into parents, translates into violence, and allows the "heroes" of society to kill without repercussion, with even black people killing black people. In the shadow of the senseless death of his friend, Coates thinks of the individual Dreamers in America as a whole system, the system that killed Prince. Thus, the Dreamers perpetuate fear and violence, and do not deserve a reprieve when it comes their way in the form of the September 11 terrorist attack.

PART II, PAGES 88–99

SUMMARY

Coates describes living in Brooklyn when Samori is young. They are very poor, but they live near Uncle Ben and his wife, Aunt Janai. Coates wants to impress upon Samori that Samori has not always had nice things, but he has always had family and friends to support him. Coates describes seeing all the white people and abundance of money in Manhattan. He especially observes how they walk, laugh, and dance without fear. He reflects on the differences with which black and white children are raised. White parents can walk their children fearless and lighthearted. Black parents tell their children to be "twice as good," as it is the only way they can rise above the struggles and constraints that bind them. Coates imagines white parents telling their children to "take twice as much."

When Samori is four, his parents take him to a preschool. Samori rushes off to play with a diverse group of children. Coates's first instinct is to stop him because Samori doesn't know anyone. But Coates feels ashamed upon realizing he is proposing that his young child should be watchful and shrewd. Samori has never been afraid of rejection, and Coates admires him for this. When he takes Samori for walks, Coates instinctually always looks out of the corner of his eye, ready to defend. He always had to change his body for others—to prepare himself for attack, to have people take him seriously, to not give the police a reason to hurt him.

Coates describes a time when he took five-year-old Samori to see a movie. Afterwards, a white woman pushes Samori because he is moving slowly, and Coates yells at her. When a man defends the woman, Coates pushes the man, who threatens to have him arrested. The incident shakes Coates because he realizes that in attempting to protect Samori, he actually endangered him. He resorted back to the fear-inspired violence of his youth to protect his son's body. Had Coates been arrested, one of Samori's first memories would have been his father being assaulted by the same police who had assaulted so many other black bodies. Coates knows that he made a mistake, and the mistakes of black men always cost them double.

Coates points out that, in his experience, people who believe they are white are obsessed with exonerating themselves from any suspicion of racism. Nobody will ever admit that they are a racist or personally know any racists, even while acting clearly racist. It is far easier for Americans to think it is their own hard work that has earned them the American Dream. While acknowledging the bad days of the past, those who believe they are white are raised to believe that those unfortunate days are over despite the evidence of the prison systems, ghettos, and police brutality. Few Americans have the courage to truly acknowledge these horrors and the fact that the country was built on the backs of slaves.

ANALYSIS

This section highlights the differences between black and white parents, which are rooted in lived experience, fear, and willful blindness to the past. As an adult living in New York City, Coates has more of an opportunity to explore beyond his neighborhood. He discovers the gap between himself and the white population, and that there exists a clear association between money, race, and fear. Simply by going from his home in Brooklyn to Manhattan, the difference in income astounds him. Most of the people spending money at restaurants are white people. White people dance without insecurity, even when they aren't good at it. White people take up the whole sidewalk walking their children, whereas Coates's mother held his hand so tightly. These white people walk and laugh with an ease of spirit. Because of both their race and their money, white parents are able to give their children the opportunity to grow up with significantly less fear. This is what Coates wants for Samori, and it is clear at the time of writing the letter that he has gone a long way to accomplishing it. But when Samori is little, Coates still finds himself walking the neighborhood with the same trepidation as when he was a child, except now he is also in charge of another human life.

Even as a parent, Coates has to constantly pay strict attention to his body language so as to convey that he is not a threat but that he is worth being taken seriously. When he lashes out at the woman at the theater who pushes Samori, his error isn't moral, but instead, lies in forgetting that he can be arrested simply by appearing threatening. This constant, indirect control over his body by white people essentially requires him to prove over and over that he ought to be counted as a person. This is the essence of needing to be "twice as good." Coates does not imagine that white children grow up having to prove their own worth and disprove suspicion. "Twice as good" is not something he wants Samori to experience, though he knows Samori will still have to understand the gap between black and white.

Everywhere he looks, Coates sees America perpetuating the Dream. He calls the reader to action by stating that people who believe they are white seem chiefly concerned with convincing themselves of their innocence, or at least making sure they appear innocent to others. As a human, it is difficult to come to grips with the knowledge that something you were raised believing is seriously flawed. Everyone learns about slaves in history books, but many people remain in denial that racism still exists, especially those who believe the mantra that America is always number one. Coates believes that Americans spring automatically to pride and making themselves look good. But simply believing that color shouldn't determine social hierarchy leaves out the more important truth: those who believe they are white still profit from the racist actions of their ancestors. Like the trap of an abusive relationship, until all Americans understand and admit that America has a truly dark and evil history and that all Americans are tied to that legacy, racism cannot be fixed.

PART II, PAGES 99–114

SUMMARY

> *Here is what I would like for you to know: in America, it is traditional to destroy the black body—it is heritage.*
>
> (See QUOTATIONS, p. 41)

Coates remembers taking Samori and his cousin Christopher to visit the Civil War battlefields of Petersburg, Shirley Plantation, and the Wilderness. He recalls a video on the fall of the Confederacy and how the end seems sad instead of jubilant. Everyone there admires the weapons, but nobody seems to think about their real and violent purpose. He tells Samori that the Civil War was about slavery and the robbery of black bodies, the "greatest material interest of the world." At that time, the slaves in America were worth about four billion dollars, and cotton was America's primary export. The family learns about Abraham Brian and his family fleeing their farm in Gettysburg to escape George Pickett. America portrays the conflict as a narrative in which both sides fight with courage and valor, obscuring the mass enslavement and murder perpetrated in the South. The Dream consists of this dishonest innocence, furthered by historians and Hollywood.

Coates wants Samori to know that America's tradition is to destroy the black body. As Coates pictures the Confederates charging the Brian farm, he sees them running toward their birthright—the right to destroy black bodies. The labor isn't "borrowed." It is violently forced. Coates launches into a chilling description of the physical atrocities committed against slaves. He quotes Senator John C. Calhoun, who says that the great divide in America is not between the rich and poor but between black and white.

While writing an article in Chicago, Coates shadows police officers as they evict a family from their home. He thinks about the weight of humiliation that the father must have borne and watches it translate into anger toward the police. During that time, he also visits some black members of the community who are over 100 years old. He knows they are the success stories, and for every one of them, there are hundreds of others who have never made it out of the ghetto. He explains how ghettos are just as much killing grounds as the ground on which Prince Jones was killed.

Coates asks Samori if he remembers accompanying Coates to work when he was thirteen. Coates had gone to interview a black mother whose boy had been shot because he wouldn't turn his music down. The killer claimed he saw a gun on the boy, though none was ever found. The man was not convicted of murder, only of firing repeatedly. The mother said that God had turned her anger into activism, and in this way, she was able to compose herself. She spoke directly to Samori and told him that he mattered, that he had a right to be himself. Coates hopes he has relayed the same message to Samori and confesses that he is still afraid. However, the constant threat of disembodiment alters everything he knows, from the violence of boys on the streets, to having to be twice as good, to having to have perfect manners in public so as not to raise suspicion.

ANALYSIS

One significant aspect of this section is how Coates emphasizes the sheer violence against slaves and how remnants of that violence are still present today. He takes Samori and his cousin to the battlefields because he wants them to understand, from an early age, that the Civil War was unapologetically fought over slaves, their own people. Despite whatever the boys will learn in school, their ancestors are viewed as nothing more than an industry to make money, and Civil War era white Americans believed it was their right to steal black bodies. To accomplish this, violence had to be involved, as it is not easy to get a living person to submit to a lifetime of torture. Coates doesn't sugarcoat this truth for Samori. Owning people involved hitting, whipping, bashing their heads, raping their women, and burning them like cattle.

For so long after slaves were "freed" and no longer monetized, the "right" of white Americans to put black Americans in their place through violence and murder persisted unchecked and encouraged. Even still, the violence continues in the streets of housing projects and through police killings. Even where there is not violence, systems that categorize black people as lower members of society abound through mass incarceration, the usage of derogatory terms, and underrepresentation in higher education, legal systems, and politics. Coates tries to explain to Samori the weight of living as a black person in America. Even as a young boy watching white America on TV, Coates felt the gap between his world and theirs, and the weight from that realization of that separation. This is nowhere more evident than on Civil War battlefield grounds. America has eulogized its Civil War as a conflict between states in which both sides were noble and brave, neglecting the reality that Confederates were fighting to keep black bodies enslaved. Coates takes Samori to these historic places in the hope that Samori does not fall into his own dream but becomes a conscious citizen of the beautiful and terrible world.

Coates's experiences of witnessing an eviction and bringing Samori to work while he interviews a woman whose child was killed for playing music too loud are two more examples of how systems in America work against black people. The eviction itself isn't necessarily racist, but it is built on a racist foundation. Coates describes this system that keeps families on the edge of financial ruin in the projects and ghettos as "elegant racism." White government plans neighborhoods full of public housing, and black people are steered toward these neighborhoods in the form of denied bank loans and realtors who make sure more desirable neighborhoods remain white. Next, the violence previously described within the ghettos make these neighborhoods dangerous, and on top of that, there is great shame associated with living in these neighborhoods. The anger that the evicted man has toward the police comes out of feeling powerless and ashamed. Thus, the main message communicated by the existence of ghettos is the inhumanity of black people. It is for this reason Coates believes they are just as much of a killing ground as the actual killing grounds of Prince Jones and the woman's son who was murdered for loud music.

PART II, PAGES 114–132

SUMMARY

Coates says he measures the progress of his life by looking back on himself as a boy in Baltimore and believing that boy would be proud of him now. Though he never masters the streets or the schools, he has his family, and he is a successful writer. He has spent his life searching to understand the gap between the world and himself. He finds joy in the constant struggle, which has reshaped his thoughts several times in his life. He has learned to question everything. However, he clarifies that studying to understand this gap doesn't classify as studying race. To explain, he describes apologizing for bumping into a black man at an airport, and the man's response—"You straight"—feels intimate because they are part of one "black" world.

In Coates's childhood, the Dream seems to be the top of American ambition. If he can just attain the life of the suburban white boys on TV, that will be enough. However, Samori's mother knows there is more to the world and wants to experience it. When she is thirty, she travels to Paris. Coates has never considered leaving America and doesn't understand why she would want to go. But when she returns, she shows him pictures of the city, and her curiosity infects Coates. He realizes that France is not just a separate world in his mind but an actual place with actual people. In retrospect, Coates sees that these bridges to other worlds are all around him.

Seven years later, Coates travels to Paris alone. He barely speaks French and is afraid as he tries to navigate French currency and trains. After getting settled, the city amazes him; it's like New York because of the diversity of the people in the streets, but he doesn't feel the ever-present fear for his body. While exploring, he feels a loneliness. Being so far removed from any American Dream, the weight of living in constant fear really hits him. Later, Coates and his family go back to Paris, along with Uncle Ben and Aunt Janai. Coates takes Samori there because he wants him to experience a life of his own, apart from the lens of fear and even apart from Coates himself. Even though France has never enslaved their ancestors, France has its own rules and history. Like America, it named its own group of people as "less than" (the Haitians, for example). That summer, Trayvon Martin's killer is acquitted, and Coates realizes that he could never escape the truth of his world, not even in France.

ANALYSIS

This section focuses on how travel impacts Coates by showing him a new world in which the color of his skin does not immediately define him in the eyes of others. The fact that Coates never considered traveling is surprising. By reading and researching so much in college, he had traveled a long way in his mind. He was amazed by and in love with the diversity and exoticism of the students at Howard. He knew that the first girl he fell in love with, from Bangladesh, entranced him, in part, because she carried a heritage from some other world. He thinks of himself as an intellectual searcher, but not as a physical traveler.

Kenyatta's trip to Paris is the beginning of a major change for Coates. He says she already knows more of the world than him and has always been compelled to see more of what the world has to offer. At the time that she travels to Paris, France is just a mental picture to Coates, like an exercise in imagination. When she returns and shows him pictures from Paris, he starts to see the city solidify and realizes that there are real people there, as real as people in his own life.

When Coates travels to Paris on his own, the trip presents a schema change. He still experiences fear as he flies partway around the world, figures out how to change money, and makes sure he gets on the right train. But after he settles into Paris, he notices a lack of the heavy fear that he has always felt about his safety. His loneliness is present but not negatively so. In this case, Coates is lonely because he is in a country he does not belong to. In his own country, he feels lonely in his constant fear for his body because he knows the history of America and that its traditions dictate that he, like all black people, is the negative part of America's equation. In the country in which he "belongs," he doesn't really belong. In Paris, in the midst of not belonging, Coates is freed from some of the mental chains that had bound him since childhood.

Due to his fears and harsh upbringing, Coates has built walls around himself to protect him and his loved ones at all costs. Even in Paris, it is hard for him to let his guard down. Consequently, he feels as though he has missed part of the experience of living by being on constant guard. While Coates wants Samori to experience a fearless life, he also needs Samori to know that being distanced from fear cannot erase the struggle he will go through. Samori still recognizes the permeating gap in America between black and white, which he perceives strongly when Michael Brown's killer is not indicted. Coates wants Samori to remember that America has always used black bodies for self-interest.

Part III, Pages 136–152

Summary

*Plunder has matured into habit and addiction; the
people who could author the mechanized death
of our ghettos, the mass rape of private prisons,
then engineer their own forgetting, must inevitably
plunder much more.*

(See QUOTATIONS, p. 42)

In the final part of his letter, Coates visits Prince Jones's mother, Dr.
Mable Jones. Dr. Jones was born into poverty in Louisiana, the same
place her ancestors had been enslaved. At four years old, she recog-
nized the same disparity between herself and the rest of the world
which Coates has explained in his letter. Coates briefly wonders
whether Samori first senses the gap after the Michael Brown shooting.

Determined to break her family's cycle of poverty, Dr. Jones
decided to become a doctor. She integrated her high school, and
while, at first, the white children teased her, by the end, they made
her class president. Dr. Jones received a full scholarship to Louisiana
State University and became the only black radiologist she knew,
which didn't bother her at all.

Coates describes Dr. Jones as a reserved, polite woman with
impeccable composure. He can see an ironclad determination in her
eyes, which reminds him of his own grandmother. Even when talking about Prince's death, her eyes well but tears don't fall. He likens
her to photos of black resisters in sit-ins during the 1960s. Their
eyes remain fixed on the horizon, as if they are summoning some
greater power to remain stoic. Dr. Jones speaks about her church, a
main source of her strength. Coates wonders whether he has missed
out on something by not believing in God.

Dr. Jones speaks of Prince, whom she calls Rocky after his grand-
father. Prince was smart and made friends easily, even as he went
to private schools with Dreamers. He was the only black student
at his magnet school in Texas. Dr. Jones gave him and his sister all
the things she didn't have, including vacations and cars. But Prince
always loved traveling over material things. Dr. Jones wanted him
to attend an Ivy League school, but he only applied to Howard. He
wanted to feel normal, not be used as a symbol or diversity par-
able. Dr. Jones describes Prince's death as being physically painful.

She says she expected that the police officer who killed him would be charged. Prince's sister is currently pregnant with a son, which scares Dr. Jones. She knows that nothing can protect his body, because one racist act is all it takes to destroy a black man.

After going back to his car, Coates thinks about how much Prince's family invested in Prince, only for it to disappear with his death. He remembers the photos from the Civil Rights Era, where black people allowed themselves to be tortured. He used to think it was shameful, but now thinks it is simply true. He says that perhaps the hope of the movement is to awaken the Dreamers so that they realize what they have done to the world. Coates describes going to Homecoming at Howard. He again sees the wide diaspora of black bodies. Coates feels as if he melts into them and no longer has the "birthmark of damnation." He describes it as a joyous moment of black power beyond the Dream.

Coates's final pages for Samori are about black power and the conversion of Dreamers. Coates feels the power in that joyous moment at Howard and believes it is what drew Prince Jones to that university. Black power is the view of America that comes from struggle and invites an understanding of the country as it truly is. It is also a deep understanding of how fragile bodies and the Dream are. Even the Dreamers can feel black power because, to feel their deepest emotions, they turn to music by black artists.

Dr. Jones predicts national doom, and Malcolm X said that the Dreamers must reap what they sow. But Coates believes this is too simplistic and that black people will reap it with them. Just like the Dreamers have plundered black bodies, they also plunder the physical earth and likely will not stop until the earth stops them. Lastly, Coates urges Samori to struggle with all his questions, but he doesn't want him to struggle for the Dreamers, only to hope or pray. They will have to learn to struggle themselves, to understand that their plunder of black bodies and the earth is the deathbed for everyone. The letter ends with Coates driving through the ghettos, feeling his old familiar fear.

ANALYSIS

Coates's visit to Prince's mother, Dr. Jones, is both revealing and tragic. He wants to know how she has kept on living in the wake of losing her only son to senseless violence. This interest in her individuality mirrors the way he thinks of the slaves, as complete people to be valued separately from one another. The world seems to have forgotten Prince Jones and his family, but Prince is always on Coates's mind, so he also thinks a lot about Prince's family. Coates's background in journalism certainly helps to give him the courage to call, visit, and interview Dr. Jones, despite having never met her. Coates and Dr. Jones relate to one another right away through their shared observance of the gap between black and white people. Coates first noticed it on TV, and she first noticed it at four years old. This gap is what propelled Dr. Jones to commit to becoming a doctor. Dr. Jones seems to have a special trait of being so excellent that people cannot help but like, or at least support, her. In four years of high school, she went from a girl who was bullied for her color to being elected class president, the highest esteem her classmates could give her.

Dr. Jones represents the epitome of being "twice as good," as black parents tell their children they must be to succeed. By doing everything to the absolute best of her ability, she achieved a medical scholarship in the same state where her ancestors were enslaved. But when Coates asks Dr. Jones if it bothers her that she is the only black doctor she knows, she seems insulted. This demonstrates how Dr. Jones has learned to rise above the "twice as good" mantra. By refusing to accept the "strangeness" of her position, she attempts to normalize the idea of a black, female radiologist.

In his way, Prince also refused to give power to the racial divide. Dr. Jones wanted him to go to an Ivy League school because he was a top student, but he only applied to Howard, a historically black university. In the wake of the Civil Rights Movement, America has tried to "right the wrong" of slavery by accepting more black students into colleges and universities. This creates a situation that turns black students into symbols of pride for the schools. In a backward way, this monetizes the black body yet again because schools use diversity as a marketing strategy. Prince just wanted to feel normal, and that is why he went to Howard, where he was one black body among many. Coates's visit to Dr. Jones is revealing because it explains how hard Dr. Jones had worked to get out of poverty and then give her family such a good life, but the tragic reality is that all this hard work and privilege wasn't enough to keep Prince from getting killed, for no reason at all. Dr. Jones still lives in fear for her new grandson, whom nobody will really be able to protect.

The last pages of the letter portray the complex mix of emotions Coates experiences as a black man in America. Coates revisits his thoughts about the nonviolent protestors, whom he used to shame for giving up their bodies so easily. When he says he wonders if the photos are just "true," he doesn't only mean that they just show what happened. He wonders instead whether the protestors knew something he doesn't. What if sanctity and security of the body never existed in the first place? The photos may have simply portrayed the world as the terrible place that it is. Coates recalls a happy moment of reveling in the black power of the Howard reunion. His eloquent description of what black power really means—an experience of great struggle that leads to great understanding—reiterates to Samori that life is truly found in the struggle. The ending warning that white plunder will kill the earth and its people seems to speak directly to the reader, who Coates is aware may well be white. The letter ends as it started, with fear, representing the ever-present cycle of violence that has been pushed on black people in America for centuries.

Important Quotations Explained

1.   *"Good intention" is a hall pass through history, a sleeping pill that ensures the Dream.*

This quotation from Part I, page 33, occurs when Coates discusses his experiences as a child in the school system. Coates sees the streets and the schools as two arms of the same beast. If a kid slips up on the streets, he will get hurt. If he fails in the schools, he will get suspended and then sent back to the streets, where he will get hurt. Then, society can give up on him without guilt and say he should have stayed in school. Collective society will remove itself from any responsibility for the child's well-being. So, when Coates says "good intention" here, he is speaking of all the people involved in the trap between the schools and the streets. His individual teachers may have had good intentions, but that doesn't help him in any macro way. The problem with good intentions is that they don't accept true responsibility. It is a passive way of justifying the large numbers of black children who fail out of school and end up on the streets.

   The second part of this quotation references "the Dream." Coates has already described the Dream as being an idealistic view of America, in which the country is helpful and innocent. He points out that nobody is going to openly say they want to keep black people on the streets. But also, nobody wants to take personal responsibility for figuring out the problem of the black ghettos. Teachers preach about personal responsibility and how it will make you into a good person and keep you out of jail, but that talk doesn't line up with America's "criminal irresponsibility," that has condoned generations of violence against black people.

2.   *It began to strike me that the point of my education was a kind of discomfort, was the process that would not award me my own especial Dream but would break all the dreams, all the comforting myths of Africa, of America, and everywhere, and would leave me only with humanity in all its terribleness.*

This quotation is from Part I, page 52, where Coates discusses attending Howard University. After spending innumerable days in the library trying to find answers to all his questions, he realizes that his questions *cannot* be answered at all. The process of learning, more often than not, just leads to more questions, theories, and opinions. Coates enters the library believing that if he could just read enough, he will find a streamlined explanation of black history starting in Africa and concluding with how white America is destroying black culture. Instead, Coates finds the authors arguing with each other, and it puts him in a state of mental chaos. Similarly, when he finds poetry and starts interacting with other poets, they constantly challenge each other's ideas. Furthermore, his teachers force him to analyze his words and thoughts instead of providing easy answers.

Coates has already spoken of the Dreamers who have a nice, tidy view of America in which they can proclaim the greatness of their country. Of course, this has never resonated with him, but while in college, he makes his own romantic Dream about Africa. He envisions Africans as nobility who were severed from their homeland. He has a mental trophy case of black heroes who were the pillars and innovators of their society. But the more he is challenged at Howard, the more Coates realizes he cannot regard all black people as noble in the same way that Americans who pay attention cannot regard all white people as noble. So, he realizes that the point of his education is to see the world as it really is, not to find concrete answers to all his questions. At the very least, he must recognize that no race or history can be regarded as wholly good. For Coates, education is about seeing the world realistically even when that means realizing that so much of humanity is terrible and confusing.

3. *I believed, and still do, that our bodies are our selves, that my soul is the voltage conducted through neurons and nerves, and that my spirit is my flesh.*

This quotation from Part II, page 79, occurs when Coates remembers Prince Jones's funeral. The pastor prays for forgiveness for the killer, but Coates thinks about how the police officer is not Prince's only killer. Coates believes that it is America's opinion that the nation has the right to destroy black bodies and has been doing it for a long time. Therefore, it is the whole country that has killed

Prince because the officer is merely a product of his nation's systemic racism.

Coates is unable to grieve in the same way as the rest of the people in the church because he is not religious, and, to him, Prince's death doesn't serve any higher purpose. Prince, like all people, was inextricably tied to his body, and when that body died, so did his spirit. The people around Coates in the church believe that not all of Prince has died. As Christians, they believe that Prince will move beyond his body into the afterlife. But Coates believes that the soul and spirit are in our physical selves. Once the body dies, there is nothing left. If the soul is electricity in neurons and nerves, and the spirit is the flesh, then destroying the body destroys all of a person. One thing Coates admires about the body is that it functions as a vessel for one's heritage. Thus, this quote is central to understanding why Coates holds the black body in such high regard—it is, in effect, holy.

4.   *Here is what I would like for you to know: in America, it is*
      traditional to destroy the black body — it is heritage.

This quotation from Part II, page 103, occurs when Coates visits Gettysburg. The stark and blunt quotation reflects the stark, deadly battlefield. Coates is thinking about slavery and how it was the central point of the Civil War. He imagines George Pickett's men charging Abraham Brian's free black community, believing that it was their birthright to steal those black men. The white soldiers believed it was their right because they had been told and shown that it was. It was traditional for them. He also thinks about how the government stole black bodies in order to monetize them. Coates is considering the fact that America was literally built on the backs of slaves. The cotton they produced was the economic powerhouse of the country.

Coates uses this quotation, in part, to emphasize the destruction that slavery really entailed. Slaves' bodies were destroyed through beatings, rape, and brandings, among other forms of torture. White people in America have enslaved and have been destroying black people for centuries. This destruction has happened for so long and with such totality that, at the time of the Civil War, many white people truly did believe it was their right to acquire slaves in the way someone acquires any other product. Through this quotation, Coates makes the point that the tradition is still true today, even if it

QUOTATIONS

doesn't involve physical enslavement. There is still mass incarceration, mass poverty, and a disproportionate number of black people arrested or murdered.

5.   *Plunder has matured into habit and addiction; the people who could author the mechanized death of our ghettos, the mass rape of private prisons, then engineer their own forgetting, must inevitably plunder much more.*

This quotation, from Part III, page 150, comes at the tail end of the book after Coates has finished visiting Dr. Jones. He thinks about how both Dr. Jones and Malcolm X believed that the white plunderers who have destroyed black people are doomed and will reap what they sow. Coates disagrees. He thinks black people will also reap what white people have sown. To plunder—meaning to take and destroy something that is not yours—is a choice. But as Coates has tried to show Samori, white plundering of black people had become so deeply ingrained in American life that Americans are now still having to actively unlearn even the smallest prejudicial thoughts. The resulting problems, like racial targeting, police beatings of black people, and mass incarceration, will take years to abate, if they will heal at all. If a tradition turns into a habit, the more difficult it is to make conscious decisions against it. And if that habit turns into an addiction, the deep effort required to overcome it will take generations.

When Coates says, "plunder much more," he is talking about the environment. He believes that white America cannot help it but continue to loot and plunder; they have become so used to plundering that they cannot stop. This isn't because white people have no moral compass at all. It is because they have become addicted to doing whatever is easiest and most useful in the short term. Following this quotation, Coates goes on to say that he's not making a prophecy, and he doesn't think white people are being paid back by the environment for what they have done to black people. White people will plunder for no reason more than "the seductiveness of cheap gasoline." Coates claims that if white America can plunder black bodies so systematically and then deny it, they are bound to destroy the world, too, and everyone will lose.

Key Facts

FULL TITLE
Between the World and Me

AUTHOR
Ta-Nehisi Coates

TYPE OF WORK
Nonfiction text

GENRE
Letter; memoir

LANGUAGE
English

TIME AND PLACE WRITTEN
New York, 2015

DATE OF FIRST PUBLICATION
2015

PUBLISHER
Penguin Random House

NARRATOR
Ta-Nehisi Coates is the author and narrator, and he speaks from his own perspective throughout the text.

POINT OF VIEW
The narrator speaks in first person subjective point of view. The book is, in part, a memoir written as a letter, so the author is the narrator, and he shares his complete thoughts and feelings. However, he only shows the actions and observable qualities of other people he writes about.

TONE
Direct, analytical

TENSE
The portions that describe past events from Coates's life are narrated in the past tense. The remainder of the text is in the present tense.

SETTING (TIME)

Variable, recounts events from childhood (1975) onward to 2015

SETTING (PLACE)

West Baltimore, Howard University in Washington, DC, and New York City

PROTAGONIST

Ta-Nehisi Coates

MAJOR CONFLICT

Coates struggles to understand how to live freely within his black body while residing in a country that enslaved his ancestors and continues to oppress black citizens.

RISING ACTION

The book does not follow a plot line with rising action that leads to a climax and falling action after. It is a series of life events and the thoughts and musings within those time periods. The author announces at the beginning that there is no resolution to his major conflict.

CLIMAX

The book does not follow a plot line with rising action that leads to a climax and falling action after. It is a series of life events and the thoughts and musings within those time periods. However, Prince Jones's death may constitute the climax.

FALLING ACTION

The book does not follow a plot line with rising action that leads to a climax and falling action after. The author announces at the beginning that there is no resolution to his major conflict.

THEMES

The façade of the American Dream; the destruction of the black body; the value of the Struggle

MOTIFS

Violence; Dreamers; fear

SYMBOLS

The Yard; Paris

FORESHADOWING

While speaking about his peers at Howard University, Coates foreshadows that Prince Jones will be killed at a young age.

Study Questions

1. Why is "the Struggle" an important concept for Coates to pass on to Samori?

Coates has spent most of his life in the midst of "the Struggle." He defines this as an emotional struggle about how to live within his body and feel free as a black man even though he lives in a country that enslaved his ancestors, and he can see that legacy all around him. Through engaging with that struggle, Coates became very well-read, and he grows up using writing to investigate his own thoughts. Unlike many people, Coates openly welcomes challenges to his thoughts. He debates and argues with his teachers and a group of like-minded poets in college. Through these debates, he realizes that the point of his education is to leave him in a state of discomfort that destroys all romanticized views of a nation or race. For a while, Coates views the African people as nobility who were separated from their roots and sees them as blameless. But he realizes that his view is similar to the way white Americans, whom he calls Dreamers, so often view America as blameless.

Above all, Coates wants Samori to be a conscious citizen, aware of the world in all its terribleness. Even as a black person, Samori might get sucked into a version of the American Dream or develop a dream of his own race as Coates did in college. Struggling with his thoughts, debating, and reading allows Coates to understand that no nation or race is blameless, and it is better to live with a realistic, if complex, understanding of history and racism. He wants the same outcome for his son, Samori, which can only come from "the Struggle." As Coates says near the beginning of his letter, he has never answered the question of how to live freely in his black body, but the search is worth it because it has girded him against the fear of disembodiment.

2. Why does Coates resent the school system as a child?

Coates sees the school system and the streets as two heads of the same beast, but, in a way, school is the worse of the two. Both institutions limit the control he has over his body. In the streets, the lack of control is evident through physical violence. If he makes a misstep with his body language or says the wrong thing, he can get hurt. Learning how to survive in school is, in many ways, more difficult. The schools only seem concerned with producing good students and that means students who stay quietly in line. Coates has extraordinary curiosity, but the schools aren't interested in the curiosities of black boys and girls. Instead, schools tell them to grow up to be good people and say that staying in school will keep them out of jail. Coates cannot understand why school is presented only as a deterrent from prison instead of as a place of learning.

In Coates's school textbooks, the only people of importance are white. There is no intellectual figure that he can relate to, so he turns to Malcom X, whose views are not presented or discussed in his school. Rather, the black heroes in school are the nonviolent protestors of the Civil Rights Movement. Coates thinks it is shameful that those people would allow themselves to be beaten. The pictures even make it seem like they enjoyed it. He can only compare the pictures with his own streets, and practicing nonviolence in the ghetto means that you might die. He doesn't understand why the schools would glorify black people that, to him, are so irrelevant and removed from his own black experience. Thus, the biggest cruelty that Coates sees within the school system is that if one doesn't do well in school, they are just sent back to the streets. And yet, if one goes to jail as a result of the streets, they are told they should have stayed in school. Both the schools and the streets seem to enforce the same trap of violence and prison.

3.   *What role does fear play in Coates's life?*

Fear is an ever-present demon for Coates. He grows up afraid because his neighborhood is violent. As a black man, he is also afraid of the police. There are so many instances of police beating or murdering black people without evidence or reason, and the killer going free. Coates recognizes early on that a black man's errors cost him double that of a white man. As a parent, Coates's fear manifests when he is afraid whenever Samori leaves him because he knows he cannot protect Samori from the world. He knows that, as a black man, Samori faces more instances of unjust violence and can be assaulted or arrested for almost anything.

In fact, Coates believes his own neighborhood is violent because of fear. He says he can see fear in every violent act and every action made to frighten others, from dramatic clothing to loud, intimidating music. Ultimately, it all stems from a fear of what was done to their ancestors. Every black person understands that their life can be taken from them easily, so they proactively do whatever possible to remain in control of their bodies, even if that means hurting others. Parents, too, are driven by fear. They know their children can be killed easily, so, for example, Coates's father beats him and says: "Either I can beat him, or the police." Beatings are done to show the children that they really have no security over their bodies.

STUDY QUESTIONS

How to Write Literary Analysis

The Literary Essay: A Step-by-Step Guide

When you read for pleasure, your only goal is enjoyment. You might find yourself reading to get caught up in an exciting story, to learn about an interesting time or place, or just to pass time. Maybe you're looking for inspiration, guidance, or a reflection of your own life. There are as many different, valid ways of reading a book as there are books in the world.

When you read a work of literature in an English class, however, you're being asked to read in a special way: you're being asked to perform *literary analysis*. To analyze something means to break it down into smaller parts and then examine how those parts work, both individually and together. Literary analysis involves examining all the parts of a novel, play, short story, or poem—elements such as character, setting, tone, and imagery—and thinking about how the author uses those elements to create certain effects.

A literary essay isn't a book review: you're not being asked whether or not you liked a book or whether you'd recommend it to another reader. A literary essay also isn't like the kind of book report you wrote when you were younger, when your teacher wanted you to summarize the book's action. A high school or college–level literary essay asks, "How does this piece of literature actually work?" "How does it do what it does?" and, "Why might the author have made the choices he or she did?"

The Seven Steps

No one is born knowing how to analyze literature; it's a skill and a process you can master. As you gain more practice with this kind of thinking and writing, you'll be able to craft a method that works best for you. But until then, here are seven basic steps to writing a well-constructed literary essay:

> *1. Ask questions*
> *2. Collect evidence*
> *3. Construct a thesis*

4. Develop and organize arguments
5. Write the introduction
6. Write the body paragraphs
7. Write the conclusion

---

1. Ask Questions

When you're assigned a literary essay in class, your teacher will often provide you with a list of writing prompts. Lucky you! Now all you have to do is choose one. Do yourself a favor and pick a topic that interests you. You'll have a much better (not to mention easier) time if you start off with something you enjoy thinking about. If you are asked to come up with a topic by yourself, though, you might start to feel a little panicked. Maybe you have too many ideas—or none at all. Don't worry. Take a deep breath and start by asking yourself these questions:

- **What struck you?** Did a particular image, line, or scene linger in your mind for a long time? If it fascinated you, chances are you can draw on it to write a fascinating essay.

- **What confused you?** Maybe you were surprised to see a character act in a certain way, or maybe you didn't understand why the book ended the way it did. Confusing moments in a work of literature are like a loose thread in a sweater: if you pull on it, you can unravel the entire thing. Ask yourself why the author chose to write about that character or scene the way he or she did, and you might tap into some important insights about the work as a whole.

- **Did you notice any patterns?** Is there a phrase that the main character uses constantly or an image that repeats throughout the book? If you can figure out how that pattern weaves through the work and what the significance of that pattern is, you've almost got your entire essay mapped out.

- **Did you notice any contradictions or ironies?** Great works of literature are complex; great literary essays recognize and explain those complexities. Maybe the title of the work seems to contradict its content (for example, the play *Happy Days* shows its two characters buried up to their waists in dirt). Maybe the main character acts one way around his or her family and a completely different way around his or her friends and associates. If you can find a way to explain a work's contradictory elements, you've got the seeds of a great essay.

At this point, you don't need to know exactly what you're going to say about your topic; you just need a place to begin your exploration. You can help direct your reading and brainstorming by formulating your topic as a *question*, which you'll then try to answer in your essay. The best questions invite critical debates and discussions, not just a rehashing of the summary. Remember, you're looking for something you can *prove or argue* based on evidence you find in the text. Finally, remember to keep the scope of your question in mind: is this a topic you can adequately address within the word or page limit you've been given? Conversely, is this a topic big enough to fill the required length?

GOOD QUESTIONS

"Are Romeo and Juliet's parents responsible for the deaths of their children?"
"Why do pigs keep showing up in Lord of the Flies?*"*
"Are Dr. Frankenstein and his monster alike? How?"

BAD QUESTIONS

"What happens to Scout in To Kill a Mockingbird?*"*
"What do the other characters in Julius Caesar *think about Caesar?"*
"How does Hester Prynne in The Scarlet Letter *remind me of my sister?"*

---

2. COLLECT EVIDENCE

Once you know what question you want to answer, it's time to scour the book for things that will help you answer the question. Don't worry if you don't know what you want to say yet—right now you're just collecting ideas and material and letting it all percolate. Keep track of passages, symbols, images, or scenes that deal with your topic. Eventually, you'll start making connections between these examples, and your thesis will emerge.

Here's a brief summary of the various parts that compose each and every work of literature. These are the elements that you will analyze in your essay and that you will offer as evidence to support your arguments. For more on the parts of literary works, see the Glossary of Literary Terms at the end of this section.

ELEMENTS OF STORY   These are the *what*s of the work—what happens, where it happens, and to whom it happens.

- **Plot:** All the events and actions of the work.

- **Character:** The people who act and are acted on in a literary work. The main character of a work is known as the *protagonist*.

- **Conflict:** The central tension in the work. In most cases, the protagonist wants something, while opposing forces (antagonists) hinder the protagonist's progress.

- **Setting:** When and where the work takes place. Elements of setting include location, time period, time of day, weather, social atmosphere, and economic conditions.

- **Narrator:** The person telling the story. The narrator may straightforwardly report what happens, convey the subjective opinions and perceptions of one or more characters, or provide commentary and opinion in his or her own voice.

- **Themes:** The main idea or message of the work—usually an abstract idea about people, society, or life in general. A work may have many themes, which may be in tension with one another.

ELEMENTS OF STYLE   These are the *how*s—how the characters speak, how the story is constructed, and how language is used throughout the work.

- **Structure and organization:** How the parts of the work are assembled. Some novels are narrated in a linear, chronological fashion, while others skip around in time. Some plays follow a traditional three- or five-act structure, while others are a series of loosely connected scenes. Some authors deliberately leave gaps in their work, leaving readers to puzzle out the missing information. A work's structure and organization can tell you a lot about the kind of message it wants to convey.

- **Point of view:** The perspective from which a story is told. In *first-person point of view*, the narrator involves himself or herself in the story. ("I went to the store"; "We watched in horror as the bird slammed into the window.") A first-person narrator is usually the protagonist of the work, but not always. In *third-person point of view*, the narrator does not participate in the story. A third-person narrator may closely follow a specific character, recounting that individual character's thoughts or experiences, or it may be what we call an *omniscient* narrator. Omniscient narrators see and know all: they can witness any event in any time or place and are privy to the inner thoughts and feelings of all characters. Remember that the narrator and the author are not the same thing!

- **Diction:** Word choice. Whether a character uses dry, clinical language or flowery prose with lots of exclamation points can tell you a lot about his or her attitude and personality.

- **Syntax:** Word order and sentence construction. Syntax is a crucial part of establishing an author's narrative voice. Ernest Hemingway, for example, is known for writing in very short, straightforward sentences, while James Joyce characteristically wrote in long, extremely complicated lines.

- **Tone:** The mood or feeling of the text. Diction and syntax often contribute to the tone of a work. A novel written in short, clipped sentences that use small, simple words might feel brusque, cold, or matter-of-fact.

- **Imagery:** Language that appeals to the senses, representing things that can be seen, smelled, heard, tasted, or touched.

- **Figurative language:** Language that is not meant to be interpreted literally. The most common types of figurative language are *metaphors* and *similes*, which compare two unlike things in order to suggest a similarity between them—for example, "All the world's a stage," or "The moon is like a ball of green cheese." (Metaphors say one thing *is* another thing; similes claim that one thing is *like* another thing.)

3. CONSTRUCT A THESIS

When you've examined all the evidence you've collected and know how you want to answer the question, it's time to write your thesis statement. A *thesis* is a claim about a work of literature that needs to be supported by evidence and arguments. The thesis statement is the heart of the literary essay, and the bulk of your paper will be spent trying to prove this claim. A good thesis will be:

- **Arguable.** "*The Great Gatsby* describes New York society in the 1920s" isn't a thesis—it's a fact.

- **Provable through textual evidence.** "*Hamlet* is a confusing but ultimately very well-written play" is a weak thesis because it offers the writer's personal opinion about the book. Yes, it's arguable, but it's not a claim that can be proved or supported with examples taken from the play itself.

- **Surprising.** "Both George and Lenny change a great deal in *Of Mice and Men*" is a weak thesis because it's obvious. A really strong thesis will argue for a reading of the text that is not immediately apparent.

- **Specific.** "Dr. Frankenstein's monster tells us a lot about the human condition" is *almost* a really great thesis statement, but it's still too vague. What does the writer mean by "a lot"? *How* does the monster tell us so much about the human condition?

GOOD THESIS STATEMENTS

Question: In *Romeo and Juliet*, which is more powerful in shaping the lovers' story: fate or foolishness?

Thesis: "Though Shakespeare defines Romeo and Juliet as 'star-crossed lovers,' and images of stars and planets appear throughout the play, a closer examination of that celestial imagery reveals that the stars are merely witnesses to the characters' foolish activities and not the causes themselves."

Question: How does the bell jar function as a symbol in Sylvia Plath's *The Bell Jar*?

Thesis: "A bell jar is a bell-shaped glass that has three basic uses: to hold a specimen for observation, to contain gases, and to maintain a vacuum. The bell jar appears in each of these capacities in *The Bell Jar*, Plath's semi-autobiographical novel, and each appearance marks a different stage in Esther's mental breakdown."

Question: Would Piggy in *The Lord of the Flies* make a good island leader if he were given the chance?

Thesis: "Though the intelligent, rational, and innovative Piggy has the mental characteristics of a good leader, he ultimately lacks the social skills necessary to be an effective one. Golding emphasizes this point by giving Piggy a foil in the charismatic Jack, whose magnetic personality allows him to capture and wield power effectively, if not always wisely."

4. Develop and Organize Arguments

The reasons and examples that support your thesis will form the middle paragraphs of your essay. Since you can't really write your thesis statement until you know how you'll structure your argument, you'll probably end up working on steps 3 and 4 at the same time. There's no single method of argumentation that will work in every context. One essay prompt might ask you to compare and contrast two characters, while another asks you to trace an image through a given work of literature. These questions require different kinds of answers and therefore different kinds of arguments. Below, we'll discuss three common kinds of essay prompts and some strategies for constructing a solid, well-argued case.

Types of Literary Essays

- **Compare and contrast**

  Compare and contrast the characters of Huck and Jim in The Adventures of Huckleberry Finn.

  Chances are you've written this kind of essay before. In an academic literary context, you'll organize your arguments the same way you would in any other class. You can either go *subject by subject* or *point by point*. In the former, you'll discuss one character first and then the second. In the latter, you'll choose several traits (attitude toward life, social status, images and metaphors associated with the character) and devote a paragraph to each. You may want to use a mix of these two approaches—for example, you may want to spend a paragraph apiece broadly sketching Huck's and Jim's personalities before transitioning to a paragraph or two describing a few key points of comparison. This can be a highly effective strategy if you want to make a counterintuitive argument—that, despite seeming to be totally different, the two characters or objects being compared are actually similar in a very important way (or vice versa). Remember that your essay should reveal something fresh or unexpected about the text, so think beyond the obvious parallels and differences.

- **Trace**

  Choose an image—for example, birds, knives, or eyes—and trace that image throughout Macbeth.

  Sounds pretty easy, right? All you need to do is read the play, underline every appearance of a knife in *Macbeth* and then list them in your essay in the order they appear, right? Well, not exactly. Your teacher doesn't want a simple catalog of examples. He or she wants to see you make *connections* between those examples—that's the difference between summarizing and analyzing. In the *Macbeth* example, think about the different contexts in which knives appear in the play and to what effect. In *Macbeth*, there are real knives and imagined knives; knives that kill and knives that simply threaten. Categorize and classify your examples to give them some order. Finally, always keep the overall effect in mind. After you choose and analyze your examples, you should come to some greater understanding about the work, as well as the role of your chosen image, symbol, or phrase in developing the major themes and stylistic strategies of that work.

- **Debate**

  Is the society depicted in 1984 *good for its citizens?*

  In this kind of essay, you're being asked to debate a moral, ethical, or aesthetic issue regarding the work. You might be asked to judge a character or group of characters *(Is Caesar responsible for his own demise?)* or the work itself (*Is Jane Eyre a feminist novel?*). For this kind of essay, there are two important points to keep in mind. First, don't simply base your arguments on your personal feelings and reactions. Every literary essay expects you to read and analyze the work, so search for evidence in the text. What do characters in *1984* have to say about the government of Oceania? What images does Orwell use that might give you a hint about his attitude toward the government? As in any debate, you also need to make sure that you define all the necessary terms before you begin to argue your case. What does it mean to be a "good" society? What makes a novel "feminist"? You should define your terms right up front, in the first paragraph after your introduction.

Second, remember that strong literary essays make contrary and surprising arguments. Try to think outside the box. In the *1984* example above, it seems like the obvious answer would be no, the totalitarian society depicted in Orwell's novel is *not* good for its citizens. But can you think of any arguments for the opposite side? Even if your final assertion is that the novel depicts a cruel, repressive, and therefore harmful society, acknowledging and responding to the counterargument will strengthen your overall case.

5. WRITE THE INTRODUCTION

Your introduction sets up the entire essay. It's where you present your topic and articulate the particular issues and questions you'll be addressing. It's also where you, as the writer, introduce yourself to your readers. A persuasive literary essay immediately establishes its writer as a knowledgeable, authoritative figure.

An introduction can vary in length depending on the overall length of the essay, but in a traditional five-paragraph essay it should be no longer than one paragraph. However long it is, your introduction needs to:

- **Provide any necessary context.** Your introduction should situate the reader and let him or her know what to expect. What book are you discussing? Which characters? What topic will you be addressing?

- **Answer the "So what?" question.** Why is this topic important, and why is your particular position on the topic noteworthy? Ideally, your introduction should pique the reader's interest by suggesting how your argument is surprising or otherwise counterintuitive. Literary essays make unexpected connections and reveal less-than-obvious truths.

- **Present your thesis.** This usually happens at or very near the end of your introduction.

- **Indicate the shape of the essay to come.** Your reader should finish reading your introduction with a good sense of the scope of your essay as well as the path you'll take toward proving your thesis. You don't need to spell out every step, but you do need to suggest the organizational pattern you'll be using.

Your introduction should not:

- **Be vague.** Beware of the two killer words in literary analysis: *interesting* and *important*. Of course, the work, question, or example is interesting and important—that's why you're writing about it!

- **Open with any grandiose assertions.** Many student readers think that beginning their essays with a flamboyant statement, such as "Since the dawn of time, writers have been fascinated by the topic of free will," makes them sound important and commanding. In fact, it sounds pretty amateurish.

- **Wildly praise the work.** Another typical mistake student writers make is extolling the work or author. Your teacher doesn't need to be told that "Shakespeare is perhaps the greatest writer in the English language." You can mention a work's reputation in passing—by referring to *The Adventures of Huckleberry Finn* as "Mark Twain's enduring classic," for example—but don't make a point of bringing it up unless that reputation is key to your argument.

- **Go off-topic.** Keep your introduction streamlined and to the point. Don't feel the need to throw in all kinds of bells and whistles in order to impress your reader—just get to the point as quickly as you can, without skimping on any of the required steps.

6. WRITE THE BODY PARAGRAPHS

Once you've written your introduction, you'll take the arguments you developed in step 4 and turn them into your body paragraphs. The organization of this middle section of your essay will largely be determined by the argumentative strategy you use, but no matter how you arrange your thoughts, your body paragraphs need to do the following:

- **Begin with a strong topic sentence.** Topic sentences are like signs on a highway: they tell the readers where they are and where they're going. A good topic sentence not only alerts readers to what issue will be discussed in the following paragraphs but also gives them a sense of what argument will be made *about* that issue. "Rumor and gossip play an important role in *The Crucible*" isn't a strong topic sentence because it doesn't tell us very much. "The community's constant gossiping creates an environment that allows false accusations to flourish" is a much stronger topic sentence—

it not only tells us what the paragraph will discuss (gossip) but how the paragraph will discuss the topic (by showing how gossip creates a set of conditions that leads to the play's climactic action).

- **Fully and completely develop a single thought.** Don't skip around in your paragraph or try to stuff in too much material. Body paragraphs are like bricks: each individual one needs to be strong and sturdy or the entire structure will collapse. Make sure you have really proven your point before moving on to the next one.

- **Use transitions effectively.** Good literary essay writers know that each paragraph must be clearly and strongly linked to the material around it. Think of each paragraph as a response to the one that precedes it. Use transition words and phrases such as *however*, *similarly*, *on the contrary*, *therefore*, and *furthermore* to indicate what kind of response you're making.

---

7. WRITE THE CONCLUSION

Just as you used the introduction to ground your readers in the topic before providing your thesis, you'll use the conclusion to quickly summarize the specifics learned thus far and then hint at the broader implications of your topic. A good conclusion will:

- **Do more than simply restate the thesis.** If your thesis argued that *The Catcher in the Rye* can be read as a Christian allegory, don't simply end your essay by saying, "And that is why *The Catcher in the Rye* can be read as a Christian allegory." If you've constructed your arguments well, this kind of statement will just be redundant.

- **Synthesize the arguments rather than summarizing them.** Similarly, don't repeat the details of your body paragraphs in your conclusion. The readers have already read your essay, and chances are it's not so long that they've forgotten all your points by now.

- **Revisit the "So what?" question.** In your introduction, you made a case for why your topic and position are important. You should close your essay with the same sort of gesture. What do your readers know now that they didn't know before? How will that knowledge help them better appreciate or understand the work overall?

- **Move from the specific to the general.** Your essay has most likely treated a very specific element of the work—a single character, a small set of images, or a particular passage. In your conclusion, try to show how this narrow discussion has wider implications for the work overall. If your essay on *To Kill a Mockingbird* focused on the character of Boo Radley, for example, you might want to include a bit in the conclusion about how he fits into the novel's larger message about childhood, innocence, or family life.

- **Stay relevant.** Your conclusion should suggest new directions of thought, but it shouldn't be treated as an opportunity to pad your essay with all the extra, interesting ideas you came up with during your brainstorming sessions but couldn't fit into the essay proper. Don't attempt to stuff in unrelated queries or too many abstract thoughts.

- **Avoid making overblown closing statements.** A conclusion should open up your highly specific, focused discussion, but it should do so without drawing a sweeping lesson about life or human nature. Making such observations may be part of the point of reading, but it's almost always a mistake in essays, where these observations tend to sound overly dramatic or simply silly.

A+ Essay Checklist

Congratulations! If you've followed all the steps we've outlined, you should have a solid literary essay to show for all your efforts. What if you've got your sights set on an A+? To write the kind of superlative essay that will be rewarded with a perfect grade, keep the following rubric in mind. These are the qualities that teachers expect to see in a truly A+ essay. How does yours stack up?

- ✓ Demonstrates a thorough understanding of the book
- ✓ Presents an original, compelling argument
- ✓ Thoughtfully analyzes the text's formal elements
- ✓ Uses appropriate and insightful examples
- ✓ Structures ideas in a logical and progressive order
- ✓ Demonstrates a mastery of sentence construction, transitions, grammar, spelling, and word choice

LITERARY ANALYSIS

Suggested Essay Topics

1. Why does Coates see Howard University as his Mecca?

2. Why does Coates refer to white Americans as "people who believe they are white"?

3. Why does Coates have trouble feeling sympathy for the first responders of 9/11?

4. How does Samori's mother change Coates?

5. How does Coates use journalism to express his views?

6. In what ways is Samori's world different than the one in which Coates grew up?

LITERARY ANALYSIS

GLOSSARY OF LITERARY TERMS

ANTAGONIST

The entity that acts to frustrate the goals of the *protagonist*. The antagonist is usually another *character* but may also be a nonhuman force.

ANTIHERO / ANTIHEROINE

A *protagonist* who is not admirable or who challenges notions of what should be considered admirable.

CHARACTER

A person, animal, or any other thing with a personality that appears in a *narrative*.

CLIMAX

The moment of greatest intensity in a text or the major turning point in the *plot*.

CONFLICT

The central struggle that moves the *plot* forward. The conflict can be the *protagonist*'s struggle against fate, nature, society, or another person.

FIRST-PERSON POINT OF VIEW

A literary style in which the *narrator* tells the story from his or her own *point of view* and refers to himself or herself as "I." The narrator may be an active participant in the story or just an observer.

HERO / HEROINE

The principal *character* in a literary work or *narrative*.

IMAGERY

Language that brings to mind sense-impressions, representing things that can be seen, smelled, heard, tasted, or touched.

MOTIF

A recurring idea, structure, contrast, or device that develops or informs the major *themes* of a work of literature.

NARRATIVE

A story.

LITERARY ANALYSIS

NARRATOR

The person (sometimes a *character*) who tells a story; the *voice* assumed by the writer. The narrator and the author of the work of literature are not the same thing.

PLOT

The arrangement of the events in a story, including the sequence in which they are told, the relative emphasis they are given, and the causal connections between events.

POINT OF VIEW

The *perspective* that a *narrative* takes toward the events it describes.

PROTAGONIST

The main *character* around whom the story revolves.

SETTING

The location of a *narrative* in time and space. Setting creates mood or atmosphere.

SUBPLOT

A secondary *plot* that is of less importance to the overall story but that may serve as a point of contrast or comparison to the main plot.

SYMBOL

An object, *character*, figure, or color that is used to represent an abstract idea or concept.

SYNTAX

The way the words in a piece of writing are put together to form lines, phrases, or clauses; the basic structure of a piece of writing.

THEME

A fundamental and universal idea explored in a literary work.

TONE

The author's attitude toward the subject or *characters* of a story or poem or toward the reader.

VOICE

An author's individual way of using language to reflect his or her own personality and attitudes. An author communicates voice through *tone*, *diction*, and *syntax*.

LITERARY ANALYSIS

A Note on Plagiarism

Plagiarism—presenting someone else's work as your own—rears its ugly head in many forms. Many students know that copying text without citing it is unacceptable. But some don't realize that even if you're not quoting directly, but instead are paraphrasing or summarizing, it is plagiarism unless you cite the source.

Here are the most common forms of plagiarism:

- Using an author's phrases, sentences, or paragraphs without citing the source

- Paraphrasing an author's ideas without citing the source

- Passing off another student's work as your own

How do you steer clear of plagiarism? You should always acknowledge all words and ideas that aren't your own by using quotation marks around verbatim text or citations like footnotes and endnotes to note another writer's ideas. For more information on how to give credit when credit is due, ask your teacher for guidance or visit www.sparknotes.com.

LITERARY ANALYSIS

REVIEW & RESOURCES

QUIZ

1. What concept does Coates believe Americans have made into a god?

   A. Social equality
   B. Democracy
   C. Economics
   D. Education

2. What does Coates's mother teach him to do at four years old?

   A. Read
   B. Play the piano
   C. Write
   D. Cook

3. What happens in the 7-Eleven parking lot when Coates is a kid?

   A. He sees someone get murdered
   B. He sees crack being exchanged
   C. Police beat him for stealing candy
   D. Another kid pulls a gun on him

4. What event makes Samori go into his room and cry?

   A. Michael Brown's killer is not indicted
   B. Coates beats him with a belt
   C. He learns of his grandmother's death
   D. He is grounded

5. What is Coates's biggest fear?

   A. That the Dreamers will never wake up
   B. Life in the ghettos
   C. Disembodiment
   D. Snakes

6.   What concept does Coates say that all the violence on the streets comes from?

    A.   Anger
    B.   Love
    C.   Fear
    D.   Both B and C

7.   Whose philosophies does Coates most closely relate to?

    A.   Martin Luther King, Jr.
    B.   Rosa Parks
    C.   Malcolm X
    D.   Bayard Rustin

8.   Which war is Coates most interested in?

    A.   The Civil War
    B.   The Revolutionary War
    C.   World War I
    D.   World War II

9.   Why does the Coates family move to New York?

    A.   Coates is hired by the *New York Times*
    B.   Samori's mother gets a job there
    C.   Coates has always loved the city
    D.   Samori liked skyscrapers as a baby

10.   What does Coates call Howard University?

    A.   The Mecca
    B.   His "bridge to other worlds"
    C.   The "black diaspora"
    D.   Both A and C

11.   What other type of writing does Coates relate to Malcolm X?

    A.   Rap
    B.   Poetry
    C.   Satire
    D.   Cookbooks

REVIEW & RESOURCES

12. Who/what is Samori named after?

   A.   An African prince
   B.   An ancient region of Africa
   C.   A resister of French colonizers
   D.   A slave ship where the slaves mutinied

13. What does the woman with the dreadlocks teach Coates?

   A.   That love can be tender
   B.   That bisexuality is normal
   C.   That love is heroic
   D.   All of the above

14. What job did Dr. Jones have?

   A.   Radiologist
   B.   Librarian
   C.   Ophthalmologist
   D.   Professional chef

15. What are the "two heads of the same beast"?

   A.   School and drugs
   B.   Streets and school
   C.   Streets and drugs
   D.   Shawn and Gus

16. What career does Coates finally choose while in college?

   A.   Journalism
   B.   Social sciences
   C.   Political science
   D.   Library sciences

17. Who kills Prince Jones?

   A.   A police officer
   B.   A student at Howard University
   C.   A gang member
   D.   The killer is unknown

18. How does Coates feel when looking out at the
    9/11 destruction?

    A.   Sympathetic toward the families of people who died
    B.   Fearful for the first responders
    C.   Cold and without sympathy
    D.   Heartbroken over the state of the world

19. Why does Coates feel bad about yelling at the woman who
    pushed Samori?

    A.   He knows he lashed out unnecessarily
    B.   He is sorry that Samori had seen him get angry
    C.   He made an error that had endangered Samori
    D.   He had hurt the woman's feelings

20. Which place has a significant impact on Coates when he
    travels there?

    A.   Milan
    B.   Paris
    C.   Salzburg
    D.   Africa

21. What is America's primary export at the outset of the
    Civil War?

    A.   Oil
    B.   Corn
    C.   Ethanol
    D.   Cotton

22. What does Coates witness in Chicago while shadowing
    police officers?

    A.   A home eviction
    B.   The police using dogs to break up a street fight
    C.   A drug raid
    D.   The bust of a street gang

REVIEW & RESOURCES

23. What emotion does Coates feel when the host of the news show asks him about hope?

   A.   Gratefulness
   B.   Irritation
   C.   Sadness
   D.   Relief

24. What resource does Coates have an unusual amount of access to as a child?

   A.   Music
   B.   Books
   C.   Computers
   D.   TV

25. What does Coates see a photo of that makes him want to travel abroad?

   A.   A river
   B.   Painted doors in Paris
   C.   A famous building
   D.   People at cafes

ANSWER KEY

1. B; 2. A; 3. D; 4. A; 5. C; 6. D; 7. C; 8. A; 9. B; 10. D; 11. B; 12. C;
13. D; 14. A; 15. B; 16. A; 17. A; 18. C; 19. C; 20. B; 21. D; 22. A;
23. C; 24. B; 25. B

Suggestions for Further Reading

Alexander, Michelle. "Ta-Nehisi Coates's 'Between The World And Me'." *New York Times*, August 17, 2015. https://www.nytimes.com/2015/08/17/books/review/ta-nehisi-coates-between-the-world-and-me.html.

Coates, Ta-Nehisi. The Black Family in the Age of Mass Incarceration." *The Atlantic*, https://www.theatlantic.com/magazine/archive/2015/10/the-black-family-in-the-age-of-mass-incarceration/403246/.

Coates, Ta-Nehisi. "The Case for Reparations." *The Atlantic*, June 2014. https://www.theatlantic.com/magazine/archive/2014/06/the-case-for-reparations/361631/.

Coates, Ta-Nehisi. "My President Was Black." *The Atlantic*, January/February 2017. https://www.theatlantic.com/magazine/archive/2017/01/my-president-was-black/508793/.

DuBois, William Edward Burghardt. *Black Reconstruction in America: An Essay toward a History of the Part which Black Folk Played in the Attempt to Reconstruct Democracy in America, 1860–1880*, edited by Henry Louis Gates Jr. Oxford: Oxford University Press, 2007.

Morrison, Toni. *The Origin of Others*, foreword by Ta-Nehisi Coates. Cambridge, MA: Harvard University Press, 2017.

Williams, Chancellor. *The Destruction of Black Civilization: Great Issues of a Race from 4500 B.C. to 2000 A.D.* Third World Press: Chicago, 1992.

REVIEW & RESOURCES

Notes

NOTES

Notes

NOTES

NOTES

NOTES

NOTES